HOMAGE TO VALLEJ(

Homage to Vallejo

edited by

CHRISTOPHER BUCKLEY

Greenhouse Review Press

Greenhouse Review Press
3965 Bonny Doon Road
Santa Cruz, CA 95060

Designed by Gary Young
Special thanks to Stephen Pollard
Cover art, "Luxembourg Gardens," by Nadya Brown

ISBN 978-0-9655239-3-6

Printed in Canada

In Memory of Donald Justice

". . . out of respect."

Introduction

Poetry comes from poetry, the best poetry is soul-making, and there is no poetry more soul-full, more distilled of the human spirit, than that of César Vallejo.

Most readers picking up this anthology do not need a lengthy introduction to Vallejo's work. For quick reference, there is the biographical essay by Clayton Eshleman in his translation of *Poemas Humanos*, and for background and insights into the origins, engines, and inspiration of Vallejo's poetry, there are Robert Bly's and John Knoepfle's essays in *Neruda and Vallejo: Selected Poems* from Bly's Seventies Press.

I first came across the poetry of César Vallejo in that Seventies Press book edited by Bly. It was work so singular, so different from everything else I had read, that I kept the book always on my desk. The combination of love, despair, hope, anger and generosity coupled with a raw but lyric argument with God, which I found in his great poem "Agape," had me trying to write my own version of that poem for years, with, of course, not a feather of success. When it came to God, Vallejo opened up, like a bad wound, the ironies and inconsistencies of a divine plan when compared to the essential evidence of the human condition ("I Am Going To Talk About Hope"). In his essay, Bly points out that Vallejo was "absolutely authentic," that his poems do not hide any part of himself, but rather expose all of his emotion, his full response. In Vallejo, there is no poetic engineering for effect. His honesty, the simple and direct human utterance marrying image to emotion in a musical, if often painful phrasing, engaged me immediately as a young man, and I expect that quality attracts many readers to Vallejo and keeps them coming back. John Knoepfle, in his essay, "Thoughts on César Vallejo," traces the source of this lyric voice to the oral tradition of the Andes, the South American Indian poets of Peru who wrote the " 'harawi,' a mystical, inward-turning complaint."

I think it difficult to match Vallejo's intensity, for it's impossible to divide his life from his poetry. He *is* the poor, and so when he writes of poverty, its grinding effect on the soul, he is speaking from immediate experience—his daily poverty in the world, the poverty of the human spirit abandoned by God. Vallejo, speaking from a personal sense of loss, still speaks for most of us. He is there on the front lines, and his encounters are witnesses for a social consciousness, a political conscience, and a metaphysical/spiritual arm-wrestling with God and fate far outside of orthodoxy. Vallejo's poems are never simply complaint, but essential spiritual questionings. His poetry embraces a common suffering and it sings out for us, and shakes a literal fist at the sky, a sky behind which God has been inattentive. And yet Vallejo, as we see in so many great poets, possesses love and generosity, and even has compassion for God: "I consecrate you, God, because you love so much; / because you never smile; because your heart / must all the time give you great pain." ("God"). Every day, every poem, it is life and death for Vallejo, and then whatever might be in the sky, or not.

Thus, many lovers of poetry come to Vallejo via life and death, through his great poem "Black Stone Lying on a White Stone." In other hands, this poem might be artifice, rendered for effect. But not in Vallejo's hands. He meant it, and his life called the cosmos into account. And so it seems reasonable that about a quarter of our poets were influenced by this hallmark Vallejo poem, and were moved to consider their own mortality, the worldly weight and/or the aesthetic consequences of their struggle. It is appropriate that this volume is dedicated to Donald Justice who was the first poet to adapt the compelling rhetoric and vision of Vallejo to his own life. In many cases, it was Justice's moving interpretation that brought poets to the original Vallejo poem. Many years ago, I brought the

Vallejo and Justice poem to class and, through the courage of a student who wrote his own poignant rendition, I tried my own. Poetry from Poetry. My friend and fellow-poet, Mark Cox—who I met at Bread Loaf after reading my version after Vallejo and Justice—turned his hand at the "Black Stone . . ." strategy, and at his suggestion I started thinking of a collection of poems that owed their inspiration to Vallejo. A few of the poems in this book are derived from the surreal experiments in *TRILCE* which Vallejo used to convey the emotional, political, and psychological extremes he was up against early in his career. Most of the work responds to the profound voice and humanity of *Poemas Humanos*. And some poems, such as those by Philip Levine, Charles Wright, and Luis Omar Salinas, take up the actual life of Vallejo, a life given completely to poetry.

These poems testify to the profound influence of Vallejo's poems on a wide range of poets and poetic sensibilities, and are their own individual testaments to the imagination and the subjects cherished in their lines. Indeed, Vallejo has inspired affection for and attachment to his particular concepts and strategies as well as stylistic experimentation in form and language. Our collective hope is that this collection of poems will be, in some small part, a witness to the great and enduring life, poetry, and soul of César Vallejo.

—CHRISTOPHER BUCKLEY

CONTENTS

NEIL AITKEN

A Winter's Day Like Any Other
after Vallejo

I will die in the fields, my body one
with the boulders and unpulled stumps,
an echo of gray against the infinite white.

It will be winter, for it is always winter in Saskatchewan,
and I will fall forward as if in prayer in a way so simple
the crows will pause before descending, unconvinced of my act.

Perhaps I will pause as well, frozen in that moment,
thinking instead of the poem I might write
on the edge of a single stalk of grain
or the narrow surface of an ice-filled ditch.

I will die six thousand miles from home,
without hearing the last train whistle
turn to a sullen moan.

I will die with no witnesses but the great expanse of sky,
the god of wintering geese, the faint trails of smoke rising
from distant farms, the chill of my own bones,
the road, the silence, the gray uneven night.

.   .   .

HAVING SPENT so much of my life outside of the country of my birth, I find Vallejo's "Black Stone Lying on a White Stone" especially compelling. There is a sense of the inevitable in Vallejo's poem, a certainty in its simplicity, which is almost heartbreaking. "These are the witnesses," he proclaims, reducing the case to a list of unanswerable facts: the Thursdays, the bones in his arms, the solitude, the rain, and the roads. In writing my poem, I also wanted to explore this sense of removal from one's home. However, as an heir of two cultures, I have two homelands: Canada and Taiwan. Even if I am at home in one, I am always on the other side of the world from the other. Like Vallejo, it is inevitable that when I die I will be far from someplace that I love.

. . .

NEIL AITKEN has spent a good portion of his life away from home. Although a Canadian by birth, he has also lived in Saudi Arabia, Taiwan, and the United States for extended periods of time. He currently resides in Riverside, California.

B. H. BOSTON

Ars Absentia

Constant alarm again today,
nothing I can't get used to.
Even the air threatens to explode,

the mined field I thread my head through,
between howls and distant sirens,
between concatenations.

Still, the hopseed's cranberry blossom,
tangle of greasewood, Toyon cherry,
patch of cactus raking the wind,

the macadamia scraping eaves
above the porch, the green gloves of the fig
changing chords at high noon,

the ant's throes under the nail of one intent—
Some things I can't do.
Some things I can.

On the white pine table, the Spider of Ash
crosses his legs, begins
to mark in his notebook.

· · ·

FOR OVER thirty years, I've been haunted by César Vallejo's "The Spider." After many recent re-readings of Vallejo's masterpiece of clarity and empathy, his ominous diagnosis of the fatally wounded spirit of the modern world, I returned to notations I'd made not long after Larry Levis's death. I like to imagine the appearance of the messenger in the last stanza of "Ars Absentia" as a gift from beyond the veil, as a blessing from both Vallejo and Larry (in whose work spiders also famously appear). The first impulses to the poem came within months of the onset of persistent noise-induced tinnitus.

. . .

B. H. BOSTON and his family have lived in San Diego, where he and his wife Marsha both teach, since Nixon fled the White House. His work has appeared in numerous magazines—including *Crazyhorse, Black Warrior Review, Poetry NOW, Western Humanities Review, The Marlboro Review, Ploughshares*—as well as in anthologies: *Down At The Santa Fe Depot, The Geography of Home,* and *How Much Earth*. A book of his poems, *Only The Living*, was published by Helix Press. He is currently managing editor of *Poetry International* at San Diego State University.

JOHN BRADLEY

We Do Not Mourn You, César Vallejo

What do you make of this clamor? I asked César Vallejo.
Eating a bowl. Of what looked like a poem. Shredded
into fact. A glass of red wine. For the journey. Perhaps
a draft. Early or late. Of *Black Stone on a White Stone*.
Shredded so that no. Future prowler could steal. From the stolen.

I do not mourn you, César Vallejo. You said into the bowl.
To the hungry scraps. Or maybe you spoke. Into your ear:
Where God was hiding. For how often God will. Hide inside
Sugar cube. Salt shaker. Arithmetic. Right here.
Right there. Too visible to be. Seen.

But do not sever your lie. I muttered thinking.
Some of the blood. In the entity referred to as. Vallejo must
Be at war with. What we call. For lack. Of a better term.
Vallejo. Neither side. Fully endorsed. By César. Vallejo
himself not fully endorsed. By either side.

Unknown all that is known. You said. Or did the white wire.
Running from the back of your head. Into the wall socket.
And back. Charge you to say. Words running into.
And out of. Your carapace. Your thorax. Your dura mater.
Your César. And of course. Your Vallejo.

. . .

I CAN THINK of no living poet whose poetry comes anywhere near the heights of Vallejo's. Vallejo's poetry had such a huge influence on me at one point that I had to finally stop reading him altogether for several years. How not to be seduced by his embrace of those who suffer, his love/hate relationship with himself, his mercurial moods, his forging of molten language. (As I write this, I can see him smiling at me with pride and derision).

.   .   .

JOHN BRADLEY'S book of poetry entitled *Love-In-Idleness* won the Washington Prize. He was the recipient of an Illinois Arts Council grant and a NEA. His collection of parables, *Add Musk Here,* was published as a co-winner of the chapbook contest by Pavement Saw Press. He is also the editor of *Atomic Ghost: Poets Respond to the Nuclear Age* (Coffee House Press). He teaches at Northern Illinois University.

CHRISTOPHER BUCKLEY

After a Theme by Vallejo, After a Theme by Justice
for Jon Veinberg

It will come for me in Florence with the evening light, and on account of the light, in early autumn before the rainstorms have arrived—when the *sfumato,* that smoke of rose and saffron, has so overrun the air that my worn heart, poor moth, will want to take up after the profligate clouds, their violet sinking toward the west. It will find me, once more extending my stay for no reason beyond the light, known far too well by the *vinaios,* in the little places for soup—on a day when I am little more than another narrow shadow on Borgo Santi Apostoli or Via delle Terme, my body dependent on a stick, but I will not be tired of this, for even though my shoulders press against the brick, and I have no clue, my eyes will be at attention, thinking that the road is still ahead.

Doubtless a Sunday with its poor excuses for an afternoon—the trattorias dark, the tourist couples gone from the goldsmiths' shops on the Ponte Vecchio. A Sunday like all the others when I've made my way early to the loggia for the open sun in the fountain, to sit again and admire the statues, those palpable, undiminished shapes, and that smooth, colossal beauty in marble-perfect clouds that saunter down each noon from Fiesole—both reminding us of a life surpassing our own, both headed one way or the other in time. And what will it matter then if I have a smoke, comforted as I will be by the company of these white choirs of air and stone, their long and brilliant reflection on it all. And earlier, at that point where the standard-bearing cart halted on its way back from battle, I will have stopped in the *mercato,* and out of respect, and again for luck, I'll have rubbed the bronze snout of the Porcillino.

Then, I will make my way by heart to the Baptistery where the symbolism of black marble pressed alongside white will not have escaped me, where I will admire once more Ghiberti's self portrait among the panels, the bald humility of his head there on the Gates of Paradise, and looking much the same, I'll envy him his dull, protracted shining. And the sun will be bright then in the camera lenses of tourists, as atop the Duomo they focus toward Giotto's Campanile—the white, green, and terra cotta marbles blanching in that aureate stream, and the shade sliding down Ghiberti's burnished doors, and the tales about this world will once more be old tales, still lacking a little in perspective just like the blue above me when it's stripped down to a red flaming along the roofs and river banks, when the surface of the Arno is brazed for an hour or so with gold, as I head up the hillside to my room in the *soggiorno*. There, I'll finally lean across the window sill and not step aside as the far clouds fade along that road on which each of us is at last alone. And I might think then of Michelangelo at ninety despairing of all the world, of all his great art, flayed as he was with God, with the knotted ropes, the sticks of time; and for a moment I, too, might think, unwittingly, that I've seen it all.

But then I may well recall my friend in a place as strange and far away as Fresno, too old, after all, to know any better than to ride his bicycle recklessly on sidewalks by the thrift shops and Basque hotels, trying the patience of folks at the fruit stands and used-book stalls, smiling his great Baltic teeth at no one he recognizes any more, pedaling slowly home past the one revival theater still showing films in black and white. I think I'll be able to picture it as he puts his feet up on his front porch, and though he's sworn it off, he'll pour himself a water glass of wine red as an autumn sun burning low through the sycamores, and for no reason better than the end of another day, he'll drink to a deep and cloudless sky.

.   .   .

IN THE EARLY 1980s, teaching at UC Santa Barbara, I brought the Justice poem along with Vallejo's "Black Stone Lying On A White Stone" in to my poetry workshop to show a great original and a great variation, and how a poem might be personal in the best sense. The poet Chad Oness was a student of mine then and he wrote a brilliant version of his own and that, alongside Vallejo and Justice, inspired my own as I went a bit further afield. The first time I read the poem was at Breadloaf, and Donald Justice was in the audience. Talking with him later, he did not object to my effort and I was very relieved.

I first read Vallejo in the early 70s in the book Robert Bly published of Vallejo and Neruda translations by James Wright and John Knoepfle and himself. "Agape" and "God" were the poems with which I was most taken, Vallejo speaking like someone with his spirit in flames, yet someone who was capable of intense empathy which gave him a deep insight into our common humanity, coupled as it is to suffering. Then I found "Black Stone Lying on a White Stone"—the Thomas Merton translation. But after a time, I came to favor the Bly and Knoepfle version as it better conveyed, to my ear, Vallejo's inventive and direct emotional rhythms.

I spent time in Florence once, enough to know a few streets, cheap restaurants and bars, the unique quality of the light, the local lore available to tourists. But I knew about Michelangelo growing old and missing his home there. I was hoping for a long life. Looking at mortality, the possibility of transcendence, the light in Florence is a not a bad backdrop. Vallejo's compelling music echoed in my mind, the cadences of an original soul—his fierce love of life, his fist raised in defiance to his fate, his love of God, nonetheless.

. . .

CHRISTOPHER BUCKLEY is the author of thirteen books of poetry and editor of several anthologies. Among other awards he has received two NEA grants in poetry, four Pushcart Prizes, and a Fulbright Award in Creative Writing. His most recent books are SKY, The Sheep Meadow Press 2004, and, with Alexander Long, A Condition of The Spirit: The Life & Work of Larry Levis, Eastern Washington University Press, 2004.

MARK COX

Grain
after Vallejo and Justice

I will die in Kansas on a cloudless day—
one of those wholesome weekends
between wheat conventions and gun shows,
glazed over with plenty.
I may simply buckle
beneath the gold-flecked eyes of a carhop,
grasp at the little window tray
and never rise again.
The living blue of the sky
will no longer glance off my body,
my lips assume the tinge of Welch's grape juice,
my food grow cold.
These will bear witness to me:
twenty distracted tee-ball players
in three different makes of minivan.
Mark Cox will be dying. I will want
to utter "ambulance" as a last word on earth,
but it will sound like "ambitious."
I will want to say "my heart"
but it will sound like "my art."
I will not want to leave you, love.
Our son, even if grown,
will be inching up the stair rail—
shin-deep in my work boots,
he will be going up
while I am going down—

and like a snapping turtle in a $2.00 butterfly net,
I will refuse the new world.
I will not want to leave my shirts emptied
over the backs of chairs,
I will not want to leave my toothbrush
leaning dry against yours,
I will have to be taken from you, love,
carried off by strong men
whose fathers sowed the grain fields around me,
it will take three of them, love,
I will remain so heavy with need for you,
so stubbornly loyal,
and even though I will be no more
than a quickly scrawled number next to the phone,
no more than a last breath not fully exhaled,
I will root myself in this earth of ours.
I will not rise through the air
nor dissolve into ground water,
I will not yearn for release
nor turn my face to the sky.
I will have to be taken on my side, love,
the way we lay together
when I was alive.

. . .

I DO NOT now remember whose poem I read first, Vallejo's or Justice's. I know I loved both: Vallejo for his tender intensity and Justice for his insistence on pace and imagery as characterization. I developed a complex exercise of guided visualization—students imagining their own final services—meant to lead them into imaginative writing about their hopes and desires. "Grain" is simply my attempt at that exercise, probably influenced by the intensity with which my students were bent over their work. I tried it in several stances, but ultimately the direct address to my wife seemed the adaptation that allowed me to extend the concept on my own terms.

.   .   .

MARK COX teaches in the creative writing department at the University of North Carolina, Wilmington. His most recent books are *Thirty-seven Years from the Stone* and *Natural Causes*, both from the University of Pittsburgh Press.

ANA DELGADILLO

In Veracruz

I will die in December,
where *el Norte's* winds
will take my spirit
in its arms back to the sea.

I will die, in my hometown
with *la Bamba,* playing,
touching the small fingertips,
hidden within my earlobes.

I will die, where the waves
are made of white skirts
rustling to a *Jarocho* playing
the *marimba* at the *Malecón.*

I will rest my head
against the split trunk
of Doña Angela's mango tree,
its fruit, struck down by lightning.

I will rest my feet
beneath the sand
where crabs pinch
the remainder of my skin.

But I will find death
beneath a blanket of music

beneath the palm trees
hovering over me
like worried mothers.

I will die with my spirit
walking lightly into the sea.

. . .

DESPITE HIS exile from Peru and life in Paris until his death one fateful
Thursday, Vallejo's poetry contains an empowering nostalgia for his homeland. It is
his nostalgia for Peru that has attracted me to his poetry, its parallelism to so many
Latinos' sentiments here in the states, to its defining homesickness that runs through
my own blood for Mexico. His poems have greatly inspired my writing, especially
"Black Stone Lying on a White Stone."

. . .

ANA DELGADILLO was born in Veracruz, Mexico and lived in Oaxaca until age
six. She then moved with her family to Arkansas where she lived until her parents'
separation. At eleven, she moved briefly back to Mexico City with her mother
and then moved to California where she has lived since. Alongside the great Latin
American writers, her main inspiration is her daughter Lilyana, for whom she records
her memories so that later she might better know her mother and her ancestry.

JOHN OLIVARES ESPINOZA

Black Hair Lying on a White Pillow

I am fourteen and I am dead.
My body lies on its side,
      As if napping during twilight.

      I am fourteen and this is the year I was
Most likely to have killed myself
Because my self-esteem was as low as
      Water running down a sidewalk,
I was ridiculed for my skinniness.
Skinny, because I could not help
If a hot lunch was always a buck more
      Than what I could afford.

I would have probably taken a mouthful
Of sleeping pills,
      Like sunflower seeds,
Instead of using a gun because it leaves a mess,
Looking much like a bloody diarrhea on a bedroom wall.
Or if I had carved my initials
      Into my wrists
The blood would have frightened me
Into calling 9-1-1.
Even if I couldn't use my fingers to dial,
I would have tried with
      My nose,
        My tongue,
          Or even my earlobe.
Only to reach a busy signal.

It would be after dinner.
After Dad came home from work,
Yelling at us like a coach
                        For not watering the pots.
After squeezing the clusters of acne
Like raspberries in front of the bathroom mirror.
After asking Alisa Vera for a date and her
                        Not even acknowledging I asked.

It would be a Thursday.
Friday would be too late to ask for a date.
And that following Friday,
                        I would be in the *Desert Sun,*
Somewhere after the front page, but before *Family Circus.*
And I would be
                   The center of attention
In high school for once.
Before all is forgotten over the weekend. I would be remembered
During the pep rally, at half-time, a memorial:
Football players holding their helmets over their hearts,
Cheerleaders holding my freshman photo over theirs—
                    Finally my face between their cleavage.

At my funeral,
My grandmother would weep,
My grandfather, stricken with Alzheimer's,
Would believe he was dead
                 And had forgotten to crawl back into the coffin.
My epitaph would read:

"Here lies John Olivares Espinoza (1978–1992):
Born the same year as *Superman: The Movie*
Was released nationwide,
Also died the same year as Superman.
Once being his hero."

It would say nothing else
                Because I had done nothing else.

God should send me now, back into time,
To stop me. If I went back, I'd bring along photos
To show myself, and I'd say,

"John, here you are in the future,
With skin as smooth as a table counter.
Here is Dad with arms wrapped around you like a scarf.
Here are the girls you will date:
Cheerleaders, models, prom queens . . .
           The ones you want now.

Then I'd show myself a picture taken with Diana,
Our temples touching together at eye level
At my brother's 18th birthday—my brother
Who would have found me lying in bed, dead,
When he was only eleven—
"This wonderful girl," I'd tell myself,
"Is worth enduring those few more heavy years."

I would show the young John a picture of
My older brother and me, at my 21st birthday,
With his arm held around my shoulder,
As we held beer in the brotherhood of lost causes.

I'd tell him
"You will become a poet.
You are to be published young
In tiny, but illuminating journals.
You are to touch many lives like doorknobs.
Yet, you are only on the beach,
And time is still an ocean before you."

After listening to myself,
Seeing the photos,

I would not believe any of it—
Because I do not believe it now.

Instead I would sit still as if waiting
For mute clouds to speak.

But, in the meantime,
I'd pour myself a cold soda,
Because it is Thursday,
Dad is home from work,
Dinner is ready,
And I have never been so hungry.

· · ·

I ADMIT WHEN I first read Robert Bly's translation of "Black Stone Lying Upon a White Stone," I didn't understand it within its context. But after I read other poets' variation on the theme, I revisited it wanting to write my own version. I still found the vision of his death haunting and the actual events that led up to it even more so. Who were these folks beating him with sticks and rope? This sounded to me like high school torment—sticks and ropes instead of spitballs and charley horses. So, instead of me prophesying my demise, I took the angle of what if I followed through offing myself like I contemplated doing so when I was fourteen. Well, not to mention the ten million other teens like me.

Though my poem had a dark opening, I was only a few lines into writing it that the poem took off into a different direction. I couldn't help but poke fun at myself. Certainly, the feelings I had then were valid, but this poem was written at a time when my life couldn't have been better: I was dating someone special, which I hadn't done in a while, and I was writing my first poems. The John at 14 seemed overly dramatic for the John at 21. Really, I ask myself, who were my witnesses then? The soda, the acne, the Thursdays . . .

"Black Hair Upon a White Pillow" was a mirror image to "Black Stone"; mine used dark humor and was about the events after an untimely death. To me now Vallejo's theme was despair and damnation, whereas my variation of the poem was about hope and salvation. None of which César had and now I wish I could give him, but didn't know how to articulate it when I first read his poem. The same way I couldn't articulate my feelings to Diana after she had read my poem and told me, "I wish I could go back and save that little boy." My response now to her, simply, but you did.

. . .

California-born JOHN OLIVARES ESPINOZA earned his MFA from Arizona State University, where he was a Paul and Daisy Soros New American Fellow. He is the author of two chapbooks: *Aluminum Times* (Swan Scythe, 2002) and *Gardeners of Eden* (Chicano Chapbook Series, 2000). "Black Hair Upon a White Pillow" appears in his manuscript, *The Date Fruit Elegies*. Presently, John teaches English at the National Hispanic University in San Jose, California.

TIMOTHY GEIGER

The Black House in Whitehouse, Ohio

Your life begins to end
when you mistakenly move
to Whitehouse, Ohio—
crossroad of flatland state-routes
where horizon becomes
a euphemism for desolation,
unlimited gray skies
under which the oak leaves
choose to grow upside-down.
Nothing holds your hand
like plain despair.
                    This is
the perfect place to leave someone
for dead. Cornfields converge
the acres into miles in all directions.
The occasional bald clearing
of a farmhouse or barnyard
where old widows plot
the next morning's chores
and crimes.
                    You thought
you were getting away,
from the city-glare and traffic-
rumble. Instead, you tend to
a broken red tractor
in the sagging barn out back—
losing one shingle, one board

at a time—and every night
the badgers come out to murder
what scurries in the otherwise
quiet country dark.

. . .

I DISCOVERED Vallejo's "Black Stone on Top of a White Stone" later, by way of Philip Levine's "Black Stone on Top of Nothing" and also from Donald justice's "Variations on a Text by Vallejo." From those poems I made the decision to read as many translations of Vallejo as I could find. Now, I not only think I understand Vallejo's rendering, I am simply in awe of it. The ability to prognosticate, Nostradamus-like, his own death, the metaphor that death represents in relation to his life, and the sordid details of the whole affair, led me to the notion of prognosticating exactly the moment in a life when it all starts to go wrong, the balance shifts, and hence, the inevitable outcome of my poem . . . badgers. No one will ever say it as clearly or as moving as Vallejo did, may we never stop trying.

. . .

TIMOTHY GEIGER is the author of the poetry collection *Blue Light Factory*, (Spoon River Poetry Press, 1999) and six chapbooks, most recently *Small Passages* (Salmon Run Press, 1995) *Einstein and the Ants* (Rondelle Press, 1995) and *Migratory Patterns* (Brandenburg Press, 1999). His work has appeared in *Poetry*, *America*, *Quarterly West*, *Third Coast*, *Heliotrope*, *The Journal* and *Mid-American Review*. He has received a Pushcart Prize XVII, a Holt, Rinehart and Winston Award, and many state and local grants in Alabama, Minnesota and Ohio. He lives in Toledo, Ohio with his wife and son, and is the proprietor of the literary fine press Aureole Press at the University of Toledo, where he teaches poetry writing and letterpress printing.

RAY GONZALEZ

Fierce God

Out of the adobe
came a dark figure
singing of the morning.
It was I in another
time where I built
the walls to stay,
but they fell into
the earthquake.

Out of the passion
of the feet and hands,
I explored the suspect,
but he died of thirst.
I remained senseless
and walked under
the arches, waited
for hands to mark
the opening in the earth,
my actions forgiven
when I found
no escape,
only the smell
of goat meat
frying in the dark
and open land.

Out of the whispers
crawled a thing

searching for water,
the animal of not
shape that swallowed
my sins

and spit them back,
the glue holding
the house up
for 500 years,
the creature drinking
from the fountain,
screaming to be heard.

Out of those cries
came a fear that
took families away,
replaced the years with
rain and moratoriums,
loves and magnitudes
fit for a wiser
and negotiating man.

When I stood alone,
The shell of the house
flowered into a body
I gave up on
centuries ago,
its beautiful hair

longer than the river
threatening my kingdom
with its human gaze.

Out of that look,
months without
a soul as the walls
of mud slapped a limit
on where I could live,
what I could see and say,
how often I emerged
from the black corner
where the altar was
erected centuries ago,
the spot where my knees
fall without prayer or
the answer that must
come from me.

. . .

MY RESPONSE TO César Vallejo rises from tracing personal and cultural history through the adobe ruins of my Southwestern home. As poets gaze across timeless landscapes, they are able to focus on certain moments that reveal universal truths as the crumbling walls of those revelations finally come down.

. . .

RAY GONZALEZ is the author of nine books of poetry, most recently *Consideration of the Guitar: New and Selected Poems*, BOA, 2005. He has published two nonfiction books, *The Underground Heart: A Return to a Hidden Landscape* and *Memory Fever*. He is also the author of two books of short stories, *The Ghost of John Wayne* and *Circling the Tortilla Dragon*. He is the editor of twelve anthologies, most recently *No Boundaries: Prose Poems by 24 American Poets*, Tupelo Press 2002. Among his many awards are a 1997 PEN/Oakland Josephine Miles Book Award, the 2003 Minnesota Book Award for Poetry, the 2003 Carr P. Collins/Texas Institute of Letters Award for Best Book of Non-fiction, a 2002 Western Heritage Award for Best Short Story, and a 2002 Latino Heritage Award in Literature.

ANNE GORRICK

Paris: Where All Thursdays Go to Die

I will have died in Paris
More than one rainy day could remember the days already written in me
Paris, where all Thursdays go to die
Because today writes down these lines
solitary on this bone road

One rainy day could already point out the days left in me
I will look at today as if Thursday died in Paris
I will cross the street to avoid a Thursday
recluse from rain and bone

The rain could already underline the days in me
I regard Thursday as if it died in Paris
Thursday set the bones in my arm against the river
bones inaccurate inside
César Vallejo is stenciled in rain

The women are dead in Paris today
I have already emphasized the days that have cared for the I
Today is Thursday in Paris dying
Because the famous today, Thursday, exists entirely of
Vallejo's arm bones

Paris, a city in elegy
Finally there is no other side to this day
The woman, the field, the place that intersects last in work
Perhaps Thursday
Already anxiety in pleasure and work
The I against Paris
Eight of the bones in my arm make up this line
The death fact peels around the lower part of difficulty
The reign of bone, eight roads secluded in Thursday

Paris comes in bone at this moment
crossing in César Vallejo, tin plated, done
in ruptured "oh" within this river Styx, this road
The way Thursday isolates the rain from bone

. . .

TO RUN FROM a burning building with language cutting into his hands. So many
lessons from Vallejo to help us endure this century, this day . . .

. . .

ANNE GORRICK has poetry published in *American Letters and Commentary,*
Fish Drum, Sulfur, GutCult, Dislocate, The Seneca Review, The Cortland Review,
Hunger Magazine and others. She is also a bookmaker who works in encaustic,
printmaking, and traditional Japanese papermaking.

LOLA HASKINS

Final

Me moriré en Paris con aguacero.

—*César Vallejo*

I will die in Tonala among the ceramic hamburgers.
I think I will have in my hand some very small
souvenirs—a duck, a doll's olla, a tiny snake.
And these will be like what I have tried to make
with grains of words fired hard. Something for
your child. And the duck will not have real wings,
but painted ones, done by the eyelashes
of dreams. And the olla will hold a comida
whose sweetness you can hardly imagine because
you cannot smell so small. And the snake
will be a good snake. When I am gone, it can
curl in your heart.

         And it will be the weather
of my abuela, whose hair brooked no white,
her Mexico, of hard skies blue as the rim
of a glass. And I will not fall. I will simply
sit down, by a little girl in ragged pink
and her friend with the dusty knees, who
are playing a game among some boxes because
at that moment, more than I have ever wanted
anything in my life, I will want to play too.

. . .

MY FIRST SEMESTER at Stanford I took a course in Literature of the Americas. At eighteen I was woefully ignorant, having read in the original only *Don Quixote,* and that both abridged and updated. I was dazzled in that class, especially by the poets Ibarbaru, Neruda, and Vallejo, especially by Vallejo because I loved how inseparable his work had been from his life. "Black Stone Lying on a White Stone" was my favorite poem of his—for its yin and yang (a representation new to me then) and its implication that the particulars of someone's death might be ultimate metaphor for his or her life. Since then, I've read and loved other Spanish-language poetry, but the rush of that first encounter has never left me.

·   ·   ·

LOLA HASKINS'S poetry has appeared in *The Atlantic Monthly, The Christian Science Monitor,* and *The London Review of Books.* Her most recent collections are *Desire Lines: New & Selected Poems* (BOA, 2004), *The Rim Benders* (Anhinga, 2001) and *Extranjera* (Story Line, 1998). Among her awards are an NEA grant, The Iowa Poetry Prize (for *Hunger,* 1993) and the Emily Dickinson/Writer Magazine Award from the Poetry Society of America.

EDWARD HIRSCH

A Walk with Vallejo in Paris

I am walking down Rue de la Paix on a Wednesday night in late August, a dusty night near the end of the month of Americans, a sad month when all the Parisians have fled south for their holiday, leaving only the tourists, and the shopkeepers, and the Algerians. It is a night when the heat of daylight somehow turns into the heat of midnight without ever passing through the liquids of dusk, a night of anger and nerves, and I am trying to decide where to get something to eat: at the soup kitchen near Place de la République where if I'm lucky and the lines aren't too long I can get a bowl of thin broth and a lecture on God in Arabic, *"le Dieu qui nous aime bien,"* or at the cafeteria of Cité Universitaire where the American students are generous, but where the guards usually chase me away. *"Nous n'avons pas besoin d'un autre Americain sans portefeuille."* We don't need another American without a wallet. So I opt for the relative safety of the Algerian soup line, though on the way I stop a man with a family to ask for money. Sometimes a man will feel generous in front of his wife and children, but this time the woman only clasps her pocketbook and he says, *"Je ne parle pas anglais."* I ask him in French. *"Je n'ai pas d'argent moi,"* he says. "And I don't speak English."

At Place de la République I discover that the thick double line extends around two solid blocks. There are so many Algerians without work in Paris that I won't be able to get inside the building until dawn. I am trying to decide what to do when suddenly I see César Vallejo with his hands thrust into his pockets standing under a street lamp. He nods to me. As I walk over to him I notice that his pants are patched with rags, there are deep holes in his shoes, and a single tear runs from his shoulder through the center of his shirt. He is so thin that I can see the post behind him by staring at his chest. "Come with me," he says. "I know a place where we call get some soup." And then: "I always feel sad for Americans when they're hungry. Everyone is desperate when they're poor, but Americans are pathetic."

We begin to walk and from then on Vallejo is always ahead of me. I have to hurry to stay with him like a small child trying to keep up with his father. Sometimes he stops abruptly to peer at something that interests him on the sidewalk. But where I see a weed he sees a muskrat; where I see a muskrat he sees the face of a woman. This doesn't seem to disturb him. "What matters is that we are both looking down," he says. "When you get lonely enough you'll see the face of a woman too."

While we walk his head is always on the ground, his hands are clenching and unclenching in his pockets. Sometimes he is silent for whole blocks, sometimes he talks to me. "There's a war going on," he says, "and I am always hungry. *J'ai toujours faim. Siempre tengo hambre.* Sometimes I think these are different things, and to tell the truth I am less frightened of hunger than of the Catholics in Spain. They're both murderers but at least hunger rises out of your own belly to strangle you. It doesn't pretend to come from God. Other times I think they are the same."

Finally Vallejo stops in front of a crowded tenement. "You go in," he says, and disappears into a lamppost. "Vallejo!" But he is gone. So I go inside and knock on the first door I can find in the dark hallway. Soon a woman comes to answer. She is very ugly and thin, even thinner than I am, even thinner than Vallejo, though not so tall, and she is wearing a tattered pink housecoat soaked in sweat. When she sees me she begins to weep. She must think I am someone else because she insists she's been waiting for me for so long, she didn't think I'd ever come, thank God I'm finally there, the children have been starving, the landlord has been threatening to throw them into the streets, and the children are so hungry, they haven't eaten in three days. And suddenly I see them behind her, a boy and a girl, tiny and naked, wrapped around their mother's legs, very frightened and excited. They are crying. At first I try to resist but the woman is persistent, she is dragging me into her apartment and soon the children have stopped crying, they are jumping on my lap, the woman is putting her arms around my neck, they are so happy I am there. And I am glad to be there. I hardly recognize myself and soon I am promising them everything: to bring food, to buy clothing, to pay the landlord, to find a job. And it is only later, when the children have gone to sleep and the woman takes off her housecoat that I see in her bruised body the eyes of Vallejo, the hungry eyes of Vallejo, and the sad face of the weeds, and the muskrats, and the war.

.   .   .

CÉSAR VALLEJO'S POETRY changed me. When I was in my 20s, I was especially moved by the agonizing poems Vallejo wrote in Paris, which I discovered in *Poemas Humanos*. I put myself to school on his deeply compassionate poetry. In "A Walk with Vallejo in Paris," a poem of poetic apprenticeship, I imagined myself walking with the master and learning about poetry—and life—from him.

.   .   .

EDWARD HIRSCH has published six books of poems: *For the Sleepwalkers* (1981), *Wild Gratitude* (1986), *The Night Parade* (1989), *Earthly Measures* (1994), *On Love* (1998), and *Lay Back The Darkness* (2003). He has also published three books of prose, including *How To Read A Poem* (1999) and *The Demon and the Angel* (2002). He is President of the Guggenheim Foundation.

RICHARD JACKSON

You Can't Get the Facts Until You Get the Fiction

The fact is that the Death I put on in the morning is
the same Love I take off each night. The fact is
that my life slips out the back door just as I arrive.
Just now, just as I tell you this, while I am looking
for a little dignity under the open wound of the sky,
I am putting down the story of the two lovers killed
on a bridge outside Mostar. And the fact is love is
as extinct as those animals painted on cave walls
in Spain. The fact is, there is not a place on earth
that needs us. All our immortal themes are sitting
on the porch with woolen blankets over their knees.
But who wants to believe this? Instead, I am looking
for the right words as if they were hidden under
my doormat like keys. I would like to be able to report
that the 9-year-old Rwandan girl did not hide under
her dead mother for hours. There are so many things
too horrible to say. And I would like to tell you
the eyes of the soldiers are sad, that despite all
this madness I can still kiss your soul, and yes,
you might say I was angry if it were not for the plain fact,
the indisputable fact, that I am filled with so much love,
so much irrational, foolish love, that I will not take
the pills or step off the bridge because of the single
fact of what you are about to say, some small act
of kindness from our words, some simple gesture that fools me
into thinking we can still fall, in times like this, in love.

· · ·

I FIRST ENCOUNTERED VALLEJO through the book by James Wright and Robert Bly way back in graduate school. And then I picked Vallejo up again in the early eighties for a short time, and found he opened up a whole new world—the logic of the absurd, the wild synesthesia, the verbal leaps, the personifications, outrageous statements, but also an incredible warmth, attention to detail and plain voice that said living in this sort of world was perfectly natural. I was amazed to follow how he got from one word or phrase to another, the whole way in which language dictates the flow of the ideas. From that point on he stayed with me and I suspect a lot of poems got their start, often unconsciously, after reading him.

There is something hypnotic about Vallejo's vision, and in the early nineties I began to pay even more attention to that political side of the poems. I had been working with a committee in Slovenia helping raise money and awareness about the war in Yugoslavia and among a number of horrific stories of unspeakable things that crossed our desks came the story of the lovers on the bridge, later picked up by journalists. In the midst of all the emphasis on larger atrocities at the time this story of two common people haunted me, the kind of people that haunted Vallejo. So the poem here began suddenly and unexpectedly as a take off on the lines from Vallejo, "The fact is that the place where I put on / my pants, is a house where / I take off my shirt." I loved the way the poem kept edging out through its qualifications and associations towards larger issues. So I began with the first three lines: it was the rhetoric of those lines that set a tone, a mood, and started to generate other images. But the language of the poem was pushing out larger than that, and later I heard the story from Rwanda. But a poem doesn't report this stuff as a journalist does, doesn't simply "witness," but transforms, and this is a major lesson from Vallejo, and soon the language of fact started to transform itself into the language of possibility, of possible hope, even love, in the midst of horror, exactly what the poem tries to assert at the end.

·　·　·

RICHARD JACKSON is the author of several award winning books of poems including *Half Lives* (Autumn House, 2005), *Heartwall* (University of Massachusetts Press Juniper Prize, 2001), *Alive All Day* (Cleveland State University Prize, 1992), and *Unauthorized Autobiography: New and Selected Poems* (The Ashland Poetry Press 2003). He has also published three chapbooks of translations of poetry, edited two Slovene poetry anthologies, and has published two critical books on American poetry. For his poetry he has been awarded a Fulbright Fellowship to the former Yugoslavia and a Guggenheim fellowship.

JANINE JOSEPH

Anilao, 1989
Where is that thing so important that it stopped being its cause? —César Vallejo

If there was one place I'd return to, I'd choose this photograph.

I'm willing to skim over the *Lady Christel* fishing boat, the cobblestone shore, and my hopeless dog paddle if I could just loaf again in waters that fanned around my bobbing head like peacock feathers. I'd allow my middle brother to slip me out of my inner tube and leave me deaf and kicking in the Pacific.

This time, I would know what squid ink felt like in my eyes, and I would stop pestering the silver and gray jelly-thing my father speared. No one would have to scold me twice.

I wouldn't ask for the next morning or for permission to go picking hermit crabs for my jam-jar aquarium. I could go without posing for pictures to send back home to my mother who was always vacuuming or hiding menthols in the toes of her flats.

I'd go back just for the bicep contest, even though my arms were never going to be as thick as my older brother's and I would always have to cheat by squeezing and bulging my baby fat up into a tiny muscle.

I'd even go straight into the coppery heat I now search for when temperatures reach the hundreds in Southern California. I've had to box myself in my car so long the only way to keep from suffocating is to open my mouth and heave the thin air, my lips sticking slightly over my dry teeth when I finally close my mouth and roll down the windows.

I just want to be led again into the waters by my father, learning the strut he used during the People's Power Revolution in 1986, my small hands pinching the side-seam of his pant leg as we backstroked on the waves together, and seeing the boat's Philippine flag from under the water as the only life we would ever know.

. . .

I FIRST CAME across the poetry of César Vallejo during my last year of college at the recommendation of a professor. Immediately, I was drawn to Vallejo's biography, particularly his experiences as an exile from Peru. However, after reading more of his poetry, I found I deeply admired his compassion for and knowledge of human suffering. Moreover, it was his use of direct and concise language in poems such as "Paris, October 1936," "Black Stone Lying on a White Stone," and "I Am Going to Talk About Hope" that has since influenced both me and my writing.

. . .

JANINE JOSEPH was born in the Philippines and lived there until the age of eight. She currently resides in Brooklyn, New York where she writes poetry and nonfiction.

DONALD JUSTICE

Variations on a Text by Vallejo
Me moriré en Paris con aguacero ...

I will die in Miami in the sun,
On a day when the sun is very bright,
A day like the days I remember, a day like other days,
A day that nobody knows or remembers yet,
And the sun will be bright then on the dark glasses of strangers
And in the eyes of a few friends from my childhood
And of the surviving cousins by the graveside,
While the diggers, standing apart, in the still shade of the palms,
Rest on their shovels, and smoke,
Speaking in Spanish softly, out of respect.

I think it will be on a Sunday like today,
Except that the sun will be out, the rain will have stopped,
And the wind that today made all the little shrubs kneel down;
And I think it will be a Sunday because today,
When I took out this paper and began to write,
Never before had anything looked so blank,
My life, these words, the paper, the gray Sunday;
And my dog, quivering under a table because of the storm,
Looked up at me, not understanding,
And my son read on without speaking, and my wife slept.

Donald Justice is dead. One Sunday the sun came out,
It shone on the bay, it shone on the white buildings,
The cars moved down the street slowly as always, so many,
Some with their headlights on in spite of the sun,
And after awhile the diggers with their shovels
Walked back to the graveside through the sunlight,

And one of them put his blade into the earth
To lift a few clods of dirt, the black marl of Miami,
And scattered the dirt, and spat,
Turning away abruptly, out of respect.

. . .

IN OUR CORRESPONDENCE about this anthology, Donald Justice had little
to say about the origins of his poem. He did, however, point out his note in *A
Donald Justice Reader* on "Variations on a Text by Vallejo" in which he modestly
gives some credit for the idea to another poet: "The Greek poet, Kostas Ouranis
(1890–1953), deserves some credit for this motif. Though I did not come across it
until years after my own version, Ouranis has a poem apparently dating from 1915,
the first line of which, in Kimon Friar's translation, reads: 'I shall die one day on a
mournful autumn twilight.'"—CB

. . .

DONALD JUSTICE died in Iowa City in 2004. He taught for many years at the
University of Iowa Writers Workshop and was one of our most important poets and
teachers. He was the recipient of many grants and prizes for his poetry including
the Pulitzer Prize for his *Selected Poems* (1979). He received the Bollingen Prize in
Poetry on 1991, and he has received grants from the Guggenheim Foundation, the
Rockefeller Foundation, and the National Endowment for the Arts. His *Collected
Poems* was published by Knopf (2004).

GEORGE KALAMARAS

Beware the Insistence of Gravity, or Upon Waking in the Body of César Vallejo

Beware the sleepless eye
opening in the corpse's forehead,
and his heart with no chest.
Beware the dark voice
of the mother who threatens her son
with the sleep of a nap, and the silence
of an eyelid in the way a cloud covers
a moving garden.
Beware the insistence of gravity.
Anything that insistent has something
to hide. Beware the secrets
of the wall
only the son of what the nail knows,
and the human whispering
the hammer holds.
Beware the holy mystery
of the brides, the other dress,
the one they do not wear,
and the drop of blood
forming, without a word,
at the widow's breast.

Beware the silence of the encyclopedias!
Beware the accent without a mouth,
the mouth with no kiss,
the kiss's sister!
Beware the bend in the blouse
of the woman who darkens sheets

with yesterday's sperm
murmuring from her vagina,
and the dream the deaf hear through
circles of in separate cities.

Beware, further, the sun
in the heat's chest, and its moon
full of sun, and the mountain of stars
that spills, quietly,
from the horse's skull.

Beware the penis crawling
on its hideous knees, and the dissolve
in the centipede's dusk.
And beware the golden look
of those who pray
as they stand on one foot.
Beware the doughnut with a center,
for only in its absence
can it truly know its circumference.
Beware the book with no words
or the words without valves,
and the persistence of the parentheses,
the loneliness articles
of clothes expire in their hang.
Beware, even, the separation
the part in the hair implies.

Beware the answer without a question!
The higher without the highest!
The lowest's response.
The way it regards what's below it
is actually above what you hear
leaping octaves in the moon's grass.
The birds should beware the music of the sky,
and the moon, the dime's embrace.
And you must beware the man
who paves the streets with yellow lines
which move both ways at once
and, at lunch, his ridiculous banana.
Beware the delight of the orange
as it enters the woman's mouth.
And the aggravation of the table
with no silverware, the cigarette
without match, the match's smoke
that appears, suddenly,
near the end of its world,
its most moist wood.

Beware the piece of skin left alone
on the vulturized body.
And the tongue of the saint
speaking in someone else's mouth.
Beware the hips
which call to you
in their dimming candles.

And careful, in kind, of swallowing
the dark scarf
on her mother's porch.
Believe, though, the woman in black.
Anyone with that much grief
has, from her navel, a white cord.

. . .

CÉSAR VALLEJO IS A MONUMENTAL influence on my poetry and on my conception of the imaginative possibilities of a poem. I've been reading him for roughly twenty-five years, having first discovered him translated in Robert Bly's *Neruda & Vallejo: Selected Poems* and in Clayton Eshleman and Jose Rubia Barcia's *The Complete Posthumous Poetry.*

Vallejo navigates a poem full of heart and mystical insight, but also of keen intellect and heightened political awareness, often accomplished through an incredible bending of syntax and an earthy surprise of image and juxtaposition. My poem draws directly upon Vallejo's great book-length poem, *Spain, Take This Cup from Me*—particularly the syntax and imagery of the litany of "Beware's" in the fourteenth section, the final stanza of which begins, "Beware, Spain, of your own Spain!" I draw as well, if indirectly, upon some of the syntax, imaginative leaps, and mystical interconnections in "Let the Millionaire Go Naked."

. . .

GEORGE KALAMARAS is Professor of English at Indiana University-Purdue University Fort Wayne and the author of three full-length books of poetry: *Even the Java Sparrows Call Your Hair* (Quale Press, 2004), *Borders My Bent Toward* (Pavement Saw Press, 2003), and *The Theory and Function of Mangoes* (Four Way Books, 2000), which won the Four Way Books Intro Series. He has also published two poetry chapbooks, *Beneath the Breath* (Tilton House, 1988) and *Heart Without End* (Leaping Mountain Press, 1986), as well as poems in numerous journals and anthologies in the United States, Canada, Greece, India, Japan, Thailand, and the United Kingdom.

JESSE LEE KERCHEVAL

Film Upon Film
for César Vallejo

I will die in Italy in October on a day I can already remember.

I will be walking the worn marble sidewalk toward
the commencement of Le Giornate del Cinema Muto, the future
a great film I am about to see projected

when a breeze off the river will raise the badge bearing my name
& I will feel familiar hands lift me
slightly off the pavement, before setting me aside.

I will die in Italy in October under a hand-tinted sunset

between receiving the program for that year's festival
& the opening night at the Teatre Zancanaro.
There, on the bridge across the river, I will fall,

in the moment between anticipating myself watching
that first film & crossing from here to there. My life
a bridge of a white projected over the river

which I will cross, one foot in the films I have seen,
the other keeping pace with the academy leader counting down
toward the moment when I will know all things

without having to view them by way of projection.
There, amid the honking of cars, will suddenly be God.
Or is it my father? & a bright light rising

from the far side of the river like a spotlight.
At the theater, the film will start without me,
the orchestra playing the newly commissioned score—

no one waiting for the entrance of this missing stranger
who is called to a new destination,
to an opening night of an entirely other sort.

I will die in Italy in October within sight of the Teatre Zancanaro

where a great film I will never see is playing.
I will fold first at the knees
as if in prayer, then at the slightly worn sprockets

of my spine, my vertebrae having had their final run
through the projector of time. When God calls,
I will not have to stay awake watching any longer,

but will have only to sink slowly down on
the smooth stone of the bridge & kiss the light

before it disappears. Before I do.

.   .   .

IN FALL 1987, when I was in Paris writing my first novel *The Museum of Happiness,* I was also reading Vallejo for the first time. I would walk through the wet streets and cemeteries where I was doing research and find the lines of "Black Stone Lying Upon a White Stone" running through my head the way a song does: "I will die in Paris, on a rainy day, / on some day I can already remember." Two years ago, when I was in Italy at Le Giornate del Cinema Muto, the silent film conference I attend, the poem came back to me. I was writing a collection of poems *Cinema Muto,* about the Giornate and silent film, and the shape of the Vallejo poem was suddenly there, a vessel. My thoughts about silent movies and my death filled it. I am not a formal poet, but I have a colleague, Ron Wallace, who wrote a sonnet each day for a year, and he said, after a while, all his early morning thoughts fell naturally into fourteen lines. In this case, the Vallejo poem worked as my form—though one, clearly, with which I took license.

.   .   .

JESSE LEE KERCHEVAL was born in France and raised in Florida. She is the author of six books including the novel *The Museum of Happiness* and the poetry collections *World as Dictionary* and *Dog Angel.* She teaches at the University of Wisconsin–Madison where she directs the Wisconsin Institute for Creative Writing.

RUTH KESSLER

After All the Wings of Birds

And what if after so many wings of birds,
the stopped bird doesn't survive—César Vallejo

But what if after all the wings of birds,
blood's soaring prophecy,
the future's inflorescence,
we too are to be pulled
down by the silent song of
falling leaves,
life's sad, empty
shoes, their savage
meekness . . .

What if after all the tidal rush,
youth's gaudy colors, love's breathless conquest,
we are to be swept by the
indifferent currents, the peeling paint of
brown kitchen cupboards, the slow demise
of wonder—
the heart, discarded by
the wayside,
hollow,
shriveled,
amnesiac
to its name . . .

·   ·   ·

ELEMENTAL, PASSIONATE, tragic, honest, but above all, human—this is how I see César Vallejo. Because he was a true artist, he had the courage to look into life's mirror and paint unflinchingly—often in mystical, always in raw colors—all the heavy blows he saw there. His native Peruvian roots and his deep concern for the suffering of his fellow men combined to infuse Vallejo's work with a unique spirit of magic humanism. And though poetry may indeed make nothing happen, in our Disneyesque, solipsistic culture his poetry matters all the more.

.   .   .

RUTH KESSLER is an Israeli poet, fiction writer and translator. She lives in Rochester, New York.

VANDANA KHANNA

Against Vallejo

I will die in Ireland on a cold day on the coast
when the sea burns against darkening rock
and the mist hangs low over hills. It will be
a Sunday because Sundays are days of rest
and worship and because I have worked
a lifetime only to have my spine ready to snap.

I have never seen Ireland, and my family
will not understand my longing for swift wind
smarting my skin, my fingernails turning
the blue of cornflowers. I will want to be burned
like a true Hindu, my soul set free of this jaded
body, this broken vase—so my skin can mist
and my bones crack, splinter like burning wood.

Vandana Khanna is dead. They will not understand
me far away from the heat and dust of Delhi, cloistered
in a damp room, my fingers stiff from writing.
This after years of thirst, years shivering under woolen
shawls brought back from Kashmir. They will not
understand you, feverish, whispering Spanish words
into my mouth because I love the way
vowels sound against your lips.

Or rather, I will die in Spain on a Sunday afternoon
when the stores have closed for the sun, men sitting
in the shade of a magnolia outside my window,

sipping from cold oranges, cut and soaked in sugar
water. I have never been to Spain, but will want
that heat, reminding me of my home. I will die
from the inside out, a fever turning my veins gray,
thighs bruising easily like fruit.

And you will spread my body out like a cool sheet,
cover my hands with henna, thread my body with beads
and no one will understand why but you, because I
have worked a lifetime and today I am tired of metaphors,
of empty leaves that rain like ash.

.   .   .

I FIRST ENCOUNTERED the poetry of César Vallejo in graduate school during
a period of time when I was trying to model my own work after other poets in an
attempt to work against my own comfort levels and old habits. I was drawn to
Vallejo as an experiment because his work seemed to express different sensibilities
than my own and yet, there was something that spoke to me and my own very
specific experience. Through Vallejo, I was able to move beyond my usual methods
of approaching a poem and thus, perhaps not work so much "Against Vallejo," but
against myself.

.   .   .

VANDANA KHANNA was born in New Delhi, India and has lived most of her
life in the United States. She attended the University of Virginia and received her
MFA from Indiana University. Her collection of poetry, *Train to Agra*, won the
Crab Orchard Review First Book Prize and was published in 2001. She currently
lives in Los Angeles, California.

JUSTIN LACOUR

Variation on Vallejo's *Black Stone on a White Stone* in the Big Easy, 1999

I will die in New Orleans in a humid slump,
The date is unarguable, marked upon my head.
Yes, I shall die in New Orleans, of that I can assure you,
With a "1-800-Fuck Me Up" in a plastic cup at Nick's Bar,
And the evening papers. Maybe on some Wednesday,
Like this one, in summer or autumn, but not
In carnival, I promise.

Wednesdays like this one, I play with verse,
Alone on the IBM compatible again, butchering words,
Then going out to give unsolicited advice to the populace,
Putting my elbows on the table to make bad jokes,
And churn and rechurn these lines.

Justin Lacour is dead, his college loans are forgotten.
The bars are hanging black wreaths, the liquor store
Might have to let someone go. They pinned him down,
Even though he cried uncle. They hit him heavy with
A whiffle bat. They hit him heavy

With a Nerf ball; the witnesses at the grave
On Wednesday, play with the Piñata,
Play the Dean Martin records, as requested,
Then turn their heads away, because
Damn, he owed them a lot of money.

. . .

I FIND "Black Stone Lying on a White Stone" a very engaging poem because of the challenges it brings for a reader, such as the sudden shift in perspective. Also, there is that feeling of certainty—"César Vallejo is dead"—and faith in the truth of the poem that makes it so effective. But most importantly for me with "Black Stone Lying on a White Stone," Vallejo creates something so personal that it invites readers to personalize it for themselves, which is one of the great things that poems can do.

.   .   .

JUSTIN LACOUR, a New Orleans native, earned his BA in English from the University of Houston, and an MFA at the University of Massachusetts–Amherst.

ERIK LESNIEWSKI

Brown Stones Under Blue Sky

I will not die in Rome, like I wanted to.
It wasn't a spectacle that flew from my mouth,
so much spittle congealed with dust, but the woman,
shredding a freshly killed chicken, sitting
on a blood-stained blanket, blazed her eyes at me
as if it was. I knew it useless to try explaining:
my illness, the rain that pelted as I walked,
the stones glistening—a birthmark of showers—
the winding streets I was lost in. And on,
through the statuary at Palazzo del Popolo,
only to arrive at Mausoleo di Augusto,
and find myself alone, against the gristled façade
that cradles Augustus' bones.
But this robust woman was working
her blade, having, on this drenched Tuesday,
followed her own roads, fashioned herself
a setting, which I interrupted.
She couldn't understand my voice,
but would have been my only witness,
and would have dismissed my death,
while the walls of Augustus' tomb crumbled—
sugar pines growing in the space between
the outer wall and the inner; no one
traveling the coarse roads that lead here,
as the rain strengthens, renewed.

. . .

HUMAN BEINGS TEND TO LOOK at death as wicked and unyielding, always approaching. My fascination with this idea has existed since the first death I experienced, my cousin on board flight 255 from Detroit bound for L.A. Although this should inform my writing, I had, directly, done nothing with it. It wasn't until my first reading of "Black Stone Lying on a White Stone" that I became aware of another view. Not morbid or obsessive, but assured and solitary, Vallejo viewed the inevitable end of a life as an acceptable condition of human existence. Since that first reading of "Black Stone Lying on a White Stone" I have come to regard the whole of Vallejo's work as a continual reminder of the work that poetry is meant to do. His views and his craft have imbued me with the love of poetry, as much as anything that I have experienced through reading.

.   .   .

ERIK LESNIEWSKI graduated from WMU with a MFA in poetry in 2003. Since then he has been everything except a writer; including a carpenter, drywaller, salesman, and currently a Catholic high school teacher at St. John's Jesuit. He lives alone with his guilt in Toledo, Ohio.

PHILIP LEVINE

Black Stone on Top of Nothing

Still sober, César Vallejo comes home and finds a black ribbon
around the apartment building covering the front door.
He puts down his cane, removes his greasy fedora, and begins
to untangle the mess. His neighbors line up behind him
wondering what's going on. A middle-aged woman carrying
a loaf of fresh bread asks him to step aside so she
can enter, ascend the two steep flights to her apartment,
and begin the daily task of preparing lunch for her Monsieur.
Vallejo pretends he hears nothing or perhaps he truly
hears nothing so absorbed is he in this odd task consuming
his late morning. Did I forget to mention that no one else
can see the black ribbon or understand why his fingers
seem so intent on unraveling what is not there? Remember
when you were only six and on especially hot days you
would descend the shaky steps to the cellar hoping at first
that someone, perhaps your mother, would gradually
become aware of your absence and feel a sudden seizure
of anxiety or terror. Of course no one noticed. Mother
sat for hours beside the phone waiting, and now and then
gazed at summer sunlight blazing through the parlor curtains
while below, cool and alone, seated on the damp concrete
you watched the same sunlight filter through the rising dust
from the two high windows. Beside the furnace a spider
worked brilliantly downward from the burned-out, overhead bulb
with a purpose you at that age could still comprehend.
1937 would last only six more months. It was a Thursday.

Rain was promised but never arrived. The brown spider worked
with or without hope, though when the dusty sunlight caught
in the web you beheld a design so perfect it remained
in your memory as a model of meaning. César Vallejo
untangled the black ribbon no one else saw and climbed
to his attic apartment and gazed out at the sullen rooftops
stretching southward toward Spain where his heart died. I know this.
I've walked by the same building year after year in late evening
when the swallows were settling noiselessly in the few sparse trees
beside the unused canal. I've come when the winter snow
blinded the distant brooding sky. I've come just after dawn,
I've come in spring, in autumn, in rain, and he was never there.

. . .

IN 1965, LIVING IN BARCELONA, I read César Vallejo's poems in Spanish for
the first time. One of my neighbors was Hardie St. Martin, the poet, translator, and
scholar of Hispanic poetry, whose mother tongue was Spanish. Instead of parsing
the poems to relieve my confusion, he told me to read them again. Before that year
was over, I knew I'd unearthed one of the great American visionaries, a man in
possession of a biblical indignation and a terrifying tenderness. Imitate him? Never.
His voice is too singular. But anyone who writes can be inspired by his daring and
his capacity for invention. One Vallejo a century is all we get, and that's enough.

. . .

Among PHILIP LEVINE'S sixteen books of poetry the most recent are *Breath*
(2004), and *The Mercy* (1999). He received the National Book Award in 1980 for
Ashes, and again in 1991 for *What Work Is*. In 1995 he was awarded the Pulitzer
Prize for *The Simple Truth*. He lives in Fresno, California and Brooklyn, New York.

LARRY LEVIS

The Crimes of the Shade Trees

Today, everyone forgave me.
No one mentioned the felony
Of my back against the oak,
Or the air I was breathing, earlier.
So it is possible I am not Levis.

I smoke and think possibly
I am the smoke—
Drifting through Omaha as smoke does,
Past the new sofas on sale.
Past the south view of the slaughterhouse,
And the shade trees flushing with light.

And it doesn't matter.
For example, if I am really
Something ordinary, a doorstep,
Or the gleaming of frost on someone's lawn
As he shaves, that would be alright.

I only mention this
To the caretaker of my absence,
Who dozes on a beige sofa.

While she knits us a bible
In which the blind remain blind,
Like shade trees, filling with light,

Each leaf feels its way out,
Each a mad bible of patience.

LARRY KNEW VALLEJO'S WORK WELL—he knew poetry well. But with Vallejo, he was especially keen. In a 1979 review he wrote of Tom Lux's "Sunday," he praises Lux's use of of the word 'also', saying, "The only other instance of the word 'also' working this powerfully, this cleanly, is in the work of Cesar Vallejo."—no doubt referencing lines toward the end of "Black Stone Lying on a White Stone." In that review, Levis also commends Lux for his sympathy and compassion, which he points out, ". . . would be worthless if Lux did not take on the 'desperations' he catalogues," poetic qualities and emotions transported from Larry's reading of Vallejo.

The opening of "The Crimes of the Shade Trees" echoes early lines in Vallejo's poem "Agape"—"Today, no one has come to inquire . . ." and, "Forgive me Lord. I have died so little!" Larry allowed, it would seem, Vallejo's tone and emotion, his humility, to be a touchstone for his own poem. And perhaps there is something of Vallejo's *Trilce* in the associative and imagistic leaps Larry makes, although a surreal influence from the Spanish language poets was common in a great deal of 1970s poetry. Like Vallejo, Larry knew the modesty of character, the weight of fate on the individual, the democracy of feeling/suffering that Vallejo took up again and again in his fierce and compassionate poetry.—C.B.

· · ·

LARRY LEVIS died in 1996, not yet 50. He was, and continues to be, one of the most original and important poets of our contemporary era. Among awards for his poetry are grants from the National Endowment for the Arts, a Guggenheim Fellowship, a Fulbright Award and a National Poetry Series selection. He was a native of Selma, California and attended Fresno State college where he met and worked with Philip Levine. He received an MA from Syracuse University and a PhD from the University of Iowa.

While at the University of Iowa he worked as a translator in the International Writing Program, where he read and translated Vallejo, Lorca, Neruda, Alberti, and other Spanish language poets in whom he developed an abiding interest. "The Crimes of the Shade Trees" appeared in Levis's second collection of poetry, *The Afterlife*, for which he won the Lamont Prize. It is also contained in *The Selected Levis*, University of Pittsburgh Press, 2000.

ALEXANDER LONG

Night Sky
after Vallejo

A clear, cool night—as the *Times* predicted.
Sleep will come if I lay my head and listen
To the waves departing again like childhood.

Yes, sleep will come if I stare long enough
Toward the floodlit lot and black steel of the fire
Escape where two teenagers kiss and feel something

I've forgotten the name of. Above their almost
Endless kissing, an entire nation of fireflies
Scatters their affection as light over asphalt.

Sunday still. Black stone sky that fills each hour,
Let it rain—it's so predictable. My yellow bones
Sing the wrong notes, it hurts some, but I listen.

Everything was possible once from that old table
Where I sat drawing shapes of asphodel and ash—
So, tell me, again, that your elegy will be rain, a poem

Of fireflies and waves washing the bodies of gulls
And lost fathers in casual swells onto the shore
Of your one and only sea, one voice making straight

And slow the path of time. No matter, I will be
Right here on a Sunday, a Sunday like this one,
Dusk-light like shimmied water blanching the alley

Into a kind of parchment, the windows staring,
The lines of laundry swaying then straightening,
Hissing lazily as they do . . . and there on the fire

Escape, the boy with the red hat, that's me, once,
With a longing for distance, more or less. More
Or less, Alexander Long is dead—he's been sitting

Out here all night thinking there would be time,
Which is also here, undulating like the shadows
Of smoke rising from his coffee, and the *Times*

Carefully folded on the small table. No one hated him,
The blurb might say, though he seemed to ignore them
As he sat shaded by the poplars, reading, his lips

Moving for someone perhaps he couldn't quite see
Yet, or simply something, with practice, he chose
To ignore. Inside the *Times*, more weather that will

Surely come, sudden-death victories and predictable
Vacancies, ink on the cloud-dull paper, flesh becoming
Words beneath the quiet demarcations of the rain.

. . .

I THINK I FOUND Vallejo via James Wright. I was in love with Wright's mid-career Deep Imagist poetry, specifically *Shall We Gather at the River.* I still am, and one poem in particular, "The Life," still frightens and amazes me. "It is the old loneliness . . ." And the white rose on the speaker's shoulder in the second stanza — where does that come from? From Vallejo, from his own "White Rose"—"I feel alright. Now / a stoical frost shines / in me." And we all know by now what effect that translating project had on Wright's poetry, on the voice alone: casual intensity, lyrical ferocity, distant intimacy. That's what I love, too, about Vallejo's "Black Stone Lying on a White Stone." Vallejo is speaking to no one; that is, everyone. All or none; all and none. With each slow and small movement of his bones, I feel him moving a mountain an inch. The poem is gentle, terrifying, wild, and quiet. The poem is on the farthest, most fragile branch that will not break, yet it's right here in my hands. I know precisely who he's talking to. The part that breaks my heart—the part that reaffirms my love—is that I can't talk back . . . but I try. It's through, and with, Vallejo that I most fully see what I've been getting myself into all these years: Poetry.

. . .

ALEXANDER LONG'S first two books—*Vigil* (New Issues Press) and *Noise* (RockWay Press)—will be published fall 2006 and winter 2006 respectively. With Christopher Buckley, he is co-editor of *A Condition of the Spirit: the Life & Work of Larry Levis* (Eastern Washington University Press, 2004). He's twice received Academy of American Poets prizes from the University of Delaware and has been nominated for a Pushcart Prize four times. His work has appeared in *Pleiades, Quarterly West, The Prose Poem: An International Journal, Third Coast, American Writers* (Charles Scribner's Sons), and elsewhere. He's a member of the writing faculty at West Chester University.

GINNY MACKENZIE

Note

I will not die in Paris.
I will not remember a blue city
or the smell of night air.

I will not die on Thursday.
Thursday, I know, is Vallejo's.
I will die on the prairie I think.

I will have removed my hat
that warm afternoon and fallen
near a bench with a plaque—

acknowledging a gift perhaps.
My funeral will not be black
or white but, rather, shades

of yellow. And those who
attend will wish I was there
to speak to them but will

understand that I was tired
and missed my parents, my
lovely aunt. And they will be

modestly happy that my last
breath was of jonquils. And they
will all know how good it feels.

.   .   .

VALLEJO IS A FREQUENT VISITOR to my poems; he just shows up, and never more so than now, perhaps to push me to the edge of "the inward and outward abyss" faced when the world and the soul are at war.

.   .   .

GINNY MACKENZIE'S poetry manuscript, *Skipstone*, was selected by judge Hilda Raz as the winner of the 2002 Backwaters Press contest, and her memoir of her father won the John Guyon literary nonfiction award from Southern Illinois University. Her poems and stories have appeared in *The Nation, The Iowa Review, Ploughshares, Agni, Boulevard, New Letters* and the *American Literary Review*.

DEREK MCKOWN

Belly of the Poet

I will die of something spastic and malignant. A bad stomach. I will die in a downtown hospital redolent of debt and antiseptic. I am a young man, and still I feel sorry for myself. Let us say then, I die in a garden with a stone bench, green vines curling around cold legs. Somewhere near an ocean please, so salt can weigh down my eyes instead of coins—I won't feel the need to persuade myself otherwise.

I want to smell orange blossoms, watch fat bees drift, buoyant with pollen. And I want to hear a child, a little girl, laugh, blowing a hurricane upon a city of red ants and imagining nothing will ever die. I want to wear a white suit, its pockets emptied—no, not quite: a photograph, to cover my heart—and of what or whom, who can say until he hears the bells beyond the burning sun?

. . .

THERE'S NOTHING LIKE A FUNERAL for someone you love to get you thinking about your own death. I started this poem five years ago after my Uncle Adolph's. He was small and light in a sky blue coffin anchored inside the perpetually earthquake-damaged San Gabriel Mission he'd struggled to maintain. It's the oldest question, at least for poets. Vain and narcissistic, certainly, but perhaps inevitable. Disgusted, I set it aside. Upon hearing of Don Justice's death, a poet and man I'd loved despite never having met him, I turned to his "Variations on a Text by Vallejo," and then returned to my own death. I gave it to Chris Buckley and Gary Young to read, and they helped quite a bit. Gary called it "creepy." I liked that. I figure it's best to be prepared.

. . .

DEREK MCKOWN is a lecturer in the Creative Writing department at the University of California Riverside. His poetry has appeared in *Quarterly West, Sentence, Defined Providence, The Pacific Review,* and *Sand Canyon Review* among other journals. He also publishes reviews and essays on contemporary poets and poetry. A book of poetry, *Arrows in Hand,* is published by Fountain Mountain Press.

VICTOR OLIVARES

Chuy Out to Sea—Cuba, 1998

Near the white sands of *Baracoa*, the gulls flew off among sea spray and the howls sung by strays to a crimson moon, and your best bet was to close your eyes as death came in a dare.

You stood on the edge of the pier, eyes closed, your long, greasy hair blowing back in a feeble gesture, back to the safety of the dunes. You needed to know what it was like to live without a care for once, as regret ticked loudly on your wrist. In the middle of June, all the young boys dove into manhood, swimming out there into the silence of waves, just far enough to wink, before returning to their street corners to eye the tourists from their park benches.

The gulls flew off somewhere, and you, Chuy, must have gone after them, further than anyone could—pushing on to find that place where the dead wait in an empty room. Did you find something only birds and maybe sailors know?

Maybe your secret lies in a seaweed bloom carried in the black beaks of terns? I think I hear it now off the coast of California, standing on the Santa Monica Pier, among the flickering lights of a merry-go-round—I could be almost certain . . . You've lived more than many of us. Suffering is always the same. Forgive me—I have grown tired of listening to the sea.

. . .

I FIRST CAME TO THE POETRY of César Vallejo as an undergraduate reading Bly's bilingual edition of Neruda and Vallejo. Vallejo's great poem "Agape" particularly made a mark on me, and later the prose poem, "I Am Going To Talk About Hope." I think my poem for Chuy takes from both of these poems—the forgiveness we all hope for our past, and the sense of loss that seems to overcome our hope. As Vallejo says in "I Am Going To Talk About Hope": "The pain I have has no explanations."

. . .

VICTOR OLIVARES was born in California of Cuban parents. He has worked at a cement manufacturing plant, as a physical rehabilitation therapist, as a quality control technician for a radio station. He works and writes in Syracuse, New York where he lives with his wife and son.

C. MIKAL ONESS

Family Violence
after Vallejo

My mother shouts that the Christmas decorations were not put on the tree correctly, nor were they put back in their boxes in the proper manner and order.

My brother's body finally became a sack of bones, and his skin peeled back yellow and brittle like old wallpaper curled from the corners of his bedroom.

My sister was lost looking for a husband who came to her like a luxurious scabbard studded with seashells. He was good to my niece—she cried in his arms and on his lap.

My father crippled his right arm in the rough of the fourteenth hole halfway through his back swing. His scream was a bark shard ripping from a live oak. When he dies I will bury that arm separately, many miles from the grave in a box made of bonefish scales.

Chauncey ran off, soldier, dog of my childhood, when my stepmother tried to honey his veins.

Grampa fainted in a vat of fruit thinking of chickens, and Gramma died holding a paring knife flecked with red onion and albacore.

Old Melly, great uncle with a card in his hat and an eight ball in his sweater, passed away as he sat on the edge of our fold-away bed drinking scotch in the morning and stuffing cigarette holders with fresh cotton.

We will all die of our drinking and fresh cotton—and somehow, César Vallejo, jaundiced brow of stone, I think you are right this time: all I do is shake the shoulders of my eternity and try to collect the bones of my fathers and mothers, carefully, so as not to cause any movement in the pile.

. . .

VALLEJO TAUGHT ME how to leverage language to clarify the emotional ambivalence that attends all experience. My favorites were "To My Brother Miguel" and "The Violence of the Hours," maybe because they mirrored some of my experiences at the time. Of course, even this linguistic and emotional dynamic short-circuits when children and families are dying in war. We need Vallejo now more than ever.

. . .

C. MIKAL ONESS is editor/publisher of Sutton Hoo Press in Winona, Minnesota. His poems have appeared in the *Iowa Review, Shenandoah, Colorado Review*, and *The Bloomsbury Review* among other journals. He has published a book of poems, *Water Becomes Bone*, with New Issues Press in 2000 as well as a chapbook, *Husks*, from Brandenberg Press.

ROBERT PHILLIPS

Variation on Vallejo's "Black Stone on a White Stone"
"Me Moriré en Paris con aquacero . . ."

I will die in Houston in the jungle heat,
in air-conditioned air. I already know the date.
I will die in Houston an amber afternoon,
a Thursday—that nothing day—in August,
that dog days month, when even the grass is depressed.

I will toy with a poem at my antique desk,
attempting something new, doing it badly,
but at least working, trying to see myself
alone, and I am, except for my Siamese cat
lying supine, soporific in a patch of sunlight.

Robert Phillips is dead. When he assayed
to extricate a book wedged in his overloaded
bookcase, the case fell upon him like a tower,
pinned him underneath in a tomb of hardbacks.
His Siamese stood by the cooling body for hours.

On the Interstate eighteen-wheelers smogged
the urban air. His wife came, said undoubtedly
he died happily, scribbling, then reaching for
a favorite book, getting through August in Houston—
the loneliness, the vaporous heat, the humility.

. . .

I FIRST READ "Black Stone Lying on a White Stone" in a book by Donald Justice, whose version of it was so witty and modern—with its variant first line, "I will die in Miami in the sun." I next encountered it in the Vallejo *Selected Poems,* translated with an essay by H. R. Hays (Sachem Press). Then one of my students produced a clever version for me. So it's been in the blood for a while.

.   .   .

ROBERT PHILLIPS'S seventh book of poems, *Circumstances Beyond Our Control* was published by the Johns Hopkins University Press.

BRADY RHOADES

Photograph Found Between the Pages of *Los Heraldos Negros*

This man, I want to call him César, but can't say, down in Lima
with a flute and a skinned chicken on his back. 1930s?
I can't say, except for this: He wears a suit, it could be wool,
with buttons on the cuffs, a kerchief in the pocket,
he's too slight for the suit, too young for the cane, which he leans on,
so serious! Circling himself, like an ailing fish.
The villagers are poor; they kill because they prize their sisters,
the back-turned roads are slick with mud.
That summer, a bird sleeps through a revolution, a tramp in a stitched dress
struts for olives and nine children starve like dogs.
César, tell us about Nativa, your mother, the fires rolling in the windows
on Hotel Street, the song whistling from your flute, in the 1930s, in a suit.
Tell us of your sorrow, tell us about the rain.

. . .

IN LOS DADOS ETERNAS, the poet says, "My God, if you had been a man,
today you would know how to be God." I picture Vallejo hidden in a bush, rifle on
his shoulder, an obtuse God in his sights, giving cover to Mankind. An assassin, a
lover. The *Los Heraldos Negros* poems are violent and kind, opposing those who
oppose humanity. One feels grateful after reading them. They caused me to look
upon his picture and reply.

. . .

BRADY RHOADES writes poetry and short stories. His work has appeared in *Red
Wheelbarrow, Slipstream, Cold Mountain Review, Amherst Review, Appalachia
Review* and other publications. He lives in Southern California and works as an
editor for the San Gabriel Valley Newspaper Group.

DOREN ROBBINS

Before and After Tampico
to Raphael Escamilla

In the middle of it all I thought I would take-off again,
go to the seaport of Tampico and continue that life
of drifting around, working my way as a cook

on a freighter to the Far East. I thought I could just
turn away from the straw through which everything bland
and everything functional swallowed

my forgettable name. I would stand in Tampico ready to leave
the Gulf of Mexico, the surf dark as burnt fat—and the whores,
absurd in their clothes that don't fit them, coming on to me

at the dock. And I would drink and eat with them while feeding
the skinny dogs prowling around the tables for scraps. And I would admire
those dogs because of their persistence, their sharp teeth, their

dexterous paws with unclipped nails. And maybe I would see
Raphael Escamilla in Tampico, that Indian face of his
more feminine than Vallejo's which was itself neither

male nor female—that face uncomplainingly driven along some
wire without a net. I would like to have seen again Raphael Escamilla
with that Indian face the clerk treated impatiently while he counted

from a roll of singles and fives that would get his last two sisters
smuggled into Mexico. Out there in Tampico, where my life would
change, I would like to see Raphael who first put the idea of

cooking on a ship in my mind, who therefore put Tampico in my mind.
Escamilla, who I was always paired with working weekends, overtime,
hustling the waitresses, pointing, hinting, and leering at what hung

to the middle of his leg. He said he would've work his way to Indonesia
if he had to, cooking on a ship—just to escape what was happening
in Morazan, to escape los diablos, to escape the university of

the Green Beret, and Immigration. I would like to have seen Raphael
Escamilla again in that moment when he was sending the money back
and he was confident—how could a man not be confident

who hid in a pile of corpses when the National Guard came busting
and poking with rifle butts cracking two of his ribs, and he laid still
not making a sound? I would like to be there watching him count

the money for his two sisters. I would kiss his face, awkwardly
the way males in my family kiss their brothers or fathers, I would kiss
him having thought I would never see him again, glad neither of us

had to end in L.A. for good—as long as it wasn't Morazan or at
the Rio Sumpul, but in the seaport of Tampico with our cook's knives
each wrapped deep in a towel—standing at the dock with the whores

in their tight audacious clothes, and the skinny dogs I admire for
their mindless tenacity, and with Escamilla as I always see him, confident
with that roll of singles and fives, confident as though what he sensed

was coming might not come—even though, I remind him again,
what's coming isn't going to take the least hesitant step
off its course.

. . .

I HAVE BEEN A READER of César Vallejo's since I was 19 when the old
Eshleman Grove Press edition first came out. In the lines here where I mention
him, I commemorate the daring of his interiority while standing witness to my
Latin American friend's human struggle, the struggle that Vallejo himself captured
with unique realism and compassion.

. . .

DOREN ROBBINS'S poetry and short fiction has appeared in over seventy
journals including *APR, Indiana Review, International Poetry, Hawaii Review, New
Letters, 5 a.m.*, and others. He has won prizes, grants and awards from *The Indiana
Review, River Styx, Literal Latte*, Passaic Poetry Center, The Loft Foundation and
The Centrum Residency Program. His most recent book of poems, *Driving Face
Down*, won The Blue Lynx Prize for 2001. A new book of poems, *At the Door with
Debussy*, will be published by Eastern Washington University Press is 2006. He is
Professor of Creative Writing/Literature at Foothill College.

WILLIAM PITT ROOT

Vallejo Was Right

There are moments for which there is no answer.

     Heart's door
battered in: only
its mirrors stand up
to invasion, reflecting the wreckage.
Somewhere a sea raises its eyeless phalanx
& soothes its way in over sand.

       Where
are the gauzy curtains with which
even a casual breeze
might have distracted columns of sunlight, & where
the shadows once
indisputably substantial?

Such empty halls hold only an echo
     vast as the last breath of
a child in whose eyes
fading expressions of frenzied
parents disappear. So

what remains?
Incorruptible mirrors, which neither cling to their
images nor lie. Which promise us,
no—
   which spare us
nothing.

.   .   .

IN THE MID-60s, early 70s, Bly's South American poets translated into cheap, slender, supercharged books rolled down the literary alley scattering a generation of lean hungry poets-to-be like bowling pins, sitting ducks, dumb clucks. "Oh," we said. Then, "OH!" *Neruda/Vallejo* was chief ice-breaker, bone-crusher. Neruda was the amiable Emperor, but Vallejo was the Emperor's touchstone, lodestone, Rosetta stone, *sine qua non*—the one in whose abyssal shadow Neruda perceived a depth he himself would never better. Vallejo: with his forehead vast and steep as an Andean cliff, his eyes aglow, his native mouth a line hard and strong as a horizon, and his tragic, sorrowing heart a tide, an undersong of raw courage.

.   .   .

WILLIAM PITT ROOT has been US/UK Exchange Artist and fellow of the Rockefeller and Guggenheim Foundations, Stanford University and the NEA. *White Boots: New & Selected Poems of the West* (2006) and *The Storm and Other Poems* (Carnegie Mellon Classic Contemporary series, 2005) follow *Trace Elements from a Recurring Kingdom* (Notable Book for 1995, *The Nation*) collecting Root's first five books. Root lives near Durango with his wife, poet Pamela Uschuk, and their cadre of animal companions. He is Poetry Editor for *CutThroat, a Journal of the Arts.*

DIXIE SALAZAR

Dusty Footsteps

Today I have been thinking
beyond the rain
of yesterday and now, beyond the weight

of little dusty thoughts tatted
into threes, a rosary of air
ticking dirty—clean—dirty—clean.

I don't mind this shapeless body
these ragged stumps—
I gave my feet away

to the crippled stars
stumbled and made a bargain
with dust.

Today I have not rotated
the mattress and beat it
free of mothy lust.

I have not rubbed all the black cups
white as bone nor polished
the dots from unrolled dice.

With feathers and fine steel
wool, I've tickled the eyes
of angels blind,

napped on the needles of tombstones,
watched the spider breath
unravel morning on my grave.

Now let the moon bulge and shrink,
the second hand steal bread
from the orphanage of Thursday.

Vallejo has come and gone
leaving muddy boots
on the stoop while footsteps

still echo from afar, and the hours
spill recklessly as rain
that falls where and when

it damn well pleases
that draws the sky and the earth
together in lazy connect the dots.

Today I have been thinking,
squandering thoughts—surely God will forgive
an old lady who forgets to brew his tea.

. . .

WHAT I ADMIRE MOST in Vallejo's poems is the sense of having it all, and damn the consequences. Being a female and half Latina, I harbor a galleon full of ambivalent feelings toward the paternal (Spanish) side of my own family. When I began this poem, it was with the idea of using the voice of Vallejo's cleaning woman, who cleaned up after him and gave him the time to write. Then I remembered that Vallejo was a very poor man who usually could barely afford food, much less a maid. But still, the cleaning woman's voice refused to be silenced, and finally, I realized that Vallejo and she had more in common than not and that gender was not as important as the soul that could come and go. I slipped into that place where light and shadows meet, where *duende* knows no gender.

. . .

DIXIE SALAZAR is a novelist, painter, and photographer as well as a poet. She teaches at California State University Fresno. Her books of poetry are *Hotel Fresno, Reincarnation of the Commonplace*, and most recently from the University of Arizona Press, *Blood Mysteries* (2003).

LUIS OMAR SALINAS

Letter too late to Vallejo

This is the letter that couldn't get to you
because you were looking for food in Paris.
To your frail October bones I phrase my lines
like spokes in your heart of silver, and condemn
loneliness, fools, idle walkers through an immense rain.
There is a crimson hue to your cloud, bloodless
in the sky and giving like a child. There is a pallor
on your forehead the years won't take away
and a huge meteor circling the night of insomnia,
and you're taciturn, a quiet constellation of grit
and hope in the vapor of one more night alone.
Your Peruvian soul grieves like a cistern in a warehouse
of love, and the toxic moody eyes of one who's seen hell
and disappeared to heaven on the arithmetic of air.
You never returned to Peru, the university where
your fervid muscles ached like stars on their way
to jail. I see your hunger and metaphysical black angels
working around you and an impulse says, "Everything
will end soon on a Thursday in the rain."

.   .   .

VALLEJO WAS A CRUCIAL MAN of letters—brilliant, taciturn, and pretty much on his own, reminding me of a doomed man with no recourse but to write and die. Back in the 60s and 70s, Vallejo had a great influence on younger poets, including me. He was a very compassionate man. In the final analysis, after all the labels, he was Christian.

. . .

A senior Chicano poet and important American poet, LUIS OMAR SALINAS is the author of many books and chapbooks. For his poetry he has received the Stanley Kunitz Award, the Earl Lyon Award, a General Electric Foundation Literary Award, and he has read at the Library of Congress. His most recent books are *Sometimes Mysteriously* (1997), *Greatest Hits* (2002) and *Elegy for Desire* (2005), University of Arizona Press).

REBECCA SEIFERLE

Oh give me your hand and draw me up from the suffering of this mysterious realm.

It's hard not to be anthropomorphic when
the Great God of the Hamsters doesn't hear
the insistent shriek of the newly born hamster
that has been forgotten by its mother
who carried off the other two. For all its feeble
struggling into life, like a red thread trying
to knot itself to her absent flesh, its not yet
open eyes are already buried in the natal nest,
while its mother runs back and forth, torn
as she is between the newly born and her other
litter—just three weeks old, the size of thumbs
and still trying to nurse—she's equally frantic
to nurse *and* wean, while the male hamster
sniffs after her already driven to mate again.
I know that life's a relentless process, uses
us up, just to make more mouths squealing
in the famined dark. Yet when my son
who's eight years old and cares so much
for each particular hamster that he knows
the number of golden hairs upon each tiny spine
and the exact wrinkle of each nose asks me to pray
for his hamster family, I say I will and I do, wondering
in which direction to turn my face, to cast my voice
into which darkness? For we ourselves
are all there is—our remedies, to buy another cage
and separate the older litter and the father,
so that the mother is restored to calm, Oh, measure

of our strength, and limits of our helplessness:

there is no other god of mercy than us upon this earth

. . .

MY HOMAGE TO Vallejo is so interwoven throughout my work, his presence—
like that "thread of indigenous blood" that he spoke of—that I find it difficult to
speak of. I have lived with his work so long, having read it for over thirty years, and
so closely, having translated it for fifteen, that his work is not so much a matter of
influence of style or manner, but a kind of interweaving of preoccupation, perspective,
feeling, a human interweaving.

Vallejo's wrestling with God in the intersections of the most mundane of realities,
his sharp characterizations and anger with human inequalities, his use of scientific
terminology and concepts to render the human in biological terms, his juxtapositions
of modes of discourse and his returning language to its inarticulate root, his
occasionally simpler poems of childhood and of feeling, have a correspondence with
my own work, though "translated" into a different time and being.

So to think of an homage to him, is a little like trying to say how I feel about someone
with whom I have lived, in some deep internal correspondence, for decades. More
consciously, I have taken from him that sense of a "human" poetry and a sense that
every word the poet writes must take a stand against oppression in all of its forms, as
if every poem must shoulder the weight of cultural inheritance which is so embedded
in the language.

. . .

REBECCA SEIFERLE'S third poetry collection, *Bitters*, was published by Copper
Canyon in 2001 and won the Western States Book Award. Her translations of Vallejo's
The Black Heralds was also published by Copper Canyon, and her translation of
Vallejo's *Trilce* was published by The Sheep Meadow Press in 1992. She is founding
editor of the online magazine of international poetry and poetry-in-translation *The
Drunken Boat*. She teaches at San Juan College in Farmington, New Mexico.

My Only Photograph of César Vallejo

Stream that doesn't taste of how we're doing,
fill me with fear.
Glorious memory, I won't go near you.
Sad, blond skeleton—hiss, hiss!

—*César Vallejo*

A direct glance, a blow and you've stopped
The tropical weddings with a fingerprint,
Red wax and sequins. Now you rest
On a park bench to watch a bird soar
Out of the plum tree—elongated, white speck
At dusk that disappears in the evening star.
You talk of the bones of your face and the soft
Spot behind the clavicle of a girl
As though the sphere of your boredom
Could make us blush.

The white bird swivels in her net.

Your constant walk into opposites, like the loss
Of the dove, isn't confusing but
Aggravating—it sticks in your throat!
The ledge of your voice rattles
The way little birds scrape their footprints
Through a windy landscape, or get lost
On the moon. Your pencil breaks.

Here, on the wall, I've pinned yellow flowers
At your knees. I call you *amorous father*
And trail you into a circus tent
Where you lift me up so I can see
The gleaming trapeze, clouded with sweat.

It swings, bodiless, from one side of air
To another. The smoky ceiling extends, *extends* . . .

Or again, *Uncle*, at your desk under a tin lamp:
You raise your spectacles to reach the one book

From your shelf with suitable pictures.
In my scuffed shoes while you spit
On the binding. It's clean enough now
For children. The boys I know

Are sitting in bars talking of you! *You,*
Their master of despair who names
The black fluid inside them, the claws
Running up their arms. They believe the rain
You died in now falls on their shoulders
And bare heads, that the trees

In the alleys are rooted in lesions
One to the other; you to them and the many
Aborted children floating out to sea.
The sea has sewn itself
To the moon and is only
Blamed in your mind
By sending *La Paloma* down as a shooting star—
Her sharp wings
As hot as the edge of your fever

That finally clears up with the weather.

IT MUST HAVE BEEN HARD being César Vallejo. Because his poems too were elusive, vibrant, and weighted with a wisdom hidden from me, I fell in love with his work as a possible parent for my own.

It was the 70s. He was Hero: Neruda, Vallejo, Celan, Ritsos, Montale—all the mysterious dark-eyed guys. I watched young male poets around me feel an impermeable tension of kinship. That was kind of annoying; I thought I knew better and could be Vallejo's poetic child myself.

I hadn't realized how much I missed him.

.   .   .

PAMELA STEWART owns and works a fiber farm in Hawley, Massachusetts. Her most recent book is *The Red Window* from the University of Georgia Press.

JON VEINBERG

Preaching for Winos

For you, who have grown tired of stumbling
through doorways, counting sighs and holding on to air,
for you, whose years have passed quickly
and whose hours stand still, who wait for tomorrow
to wash out the fumes and sewer stink of the shirt
you slept in, I will tie the shoe no one else would claim.

I will shadow your soul as you tiptoe
past the guard dogs roaming the used car lots,
and the store clerks scrubbing *death is forever*
graffiti off their windows and the bail jumper shuffling
his losses, past the paramedics making their rounds
and children in bowed apartment buildings

popping their knuckles, scavenging for razor blades,
and flattening pennies into quarters on railroad tracks.
For you, whose hallways I have loitered,
whose libraries I have chewed my wrists in, whose wall
I have leaned my fists against to fight sleep—
because in my dreams there were no oceans,—

no angel to slide the rent through the wind-sawed door.
The gardens of childhood went to seed,
white lightning out of kilter down the alley
and through the night under the neon's cruel wink,
beneath the smell of bacon grease floating
from the projects and the loan shark trimming his nails

on the star-blocked fire escape, the flies in frenzy,
and the luckless streetwalker staring into the mist
of headlights and dead nights, and the bookmaker
working overtime, and the crack house keeping its light
on for fresh runaways who dream of a world to behold
other than this one. For you, who are destined to die

at bus stops hugging your knees and blowing on your hands,
for you, who have asked for forgiveness
and gotten 7-day lockdowns and bitten ears in fights
over stolen batteries and cheap rides,
I will dance on my knees to save you. I will place my hand
in yours. It will be a collision of flesh. Hell will close its eye

if you listen as I coax fire back into your dead eyes.
For you, they have boarded up the health clinics
and invented deadbolts for confessionals and food banks,
for you, I have brought oranges and an umbrella
to draw out the hunger you were born into. I am here
to make your suffering matter. I am here to rewrite your epitaph.

· · ·

WHEN I FIRST READ VALLEJO as a beginning poetry student in 1972, I was most affected by his sharp-edged compassion and a genuine brutal beauty. It was as if he had dipped his pen into an ink of fire. I felt I had discovered a poet who could be personal and worldly, wise and wild, all in the same breath—a poet who had an absolute fearlessness in not just tapping, but attacking, the huge reservoir of his intuition.

I still carry some of these poems with me, within me that is. But what's more important, I carry an attitude that's forever drumming: a poem is never as good as it should be without an urgent sense of the human element—a poem should refuse to be trapped in corners. It should continue to burn and be read beyond the page.

.   .   .

JON VEINBERG lives in Fresno, California. He is the author of *An Owl's Landscape* and *Oarless Boats, Vacant Lots*. His work has been included in numerous journals and anthologies, and he has twice been the recipient of grants in poetry from the National Endowment for the Arts.

DAVID WOJAHN

Ode to 196–
after Vallejo

A girl runs toward us her napalmed back in flame.
After that we practice cursive?

A girl at her desk picks the scab, her school TB test.
And now let's babble Reichian Freudian my mother naps beside me?

Involuntary memory tonsils pruned and swimming in a jar.
Do I talk now Yogi Berra with the surgeon?

And coldest winter: Plath with her ear to the oven door.
Did I switch the channel then to more cartoons?

Footage Tet and Congo Bay of Pigs. Gunshot of course to temple.
Do I meditate on gin glass, raised nine times to my father's lips?

A garbage dump in Rio and a woman digging soup bones rinds.
How in the vestry do I pin my altar boy robes?

Hendrix Mekong Khe Sanh gasolined to fire.
Do I write now on a greeting card my first bad poem?

The candidate cradled, Sirhan Sirhan beamed by Telstar.
How talk of my father's future face, O_2 tank and blotches?

Matchbook on the table at Lorraine Hotel Shoot Out the Lights.
How talk now of L at nine, thirty years exactly more to live?

L in the schoolroom picks her scab and Newark snows.
And to speak now me thirteen, my first reeling drunk?

L in the schoolroom picks her scab and Newark burns.
Do I laugh now at Manson's shaved-headed girls?

Oswald in the kitchen cleaning rifle.
Do I study now Zapruder Number Three One Three?

Someone switches the channel more cartoons.
How speak of the I and not-I without screaming?

Of the I and not-I screaming in their nullifying unison?

. . .

"ODE" IS MODELED on the structure of Vallejo's "A Man Walks By With a Loaf of Bread on His Shoulder," which is half-sermon, half-outcry, in this case bewailing the almost unbridgeable distance between the solipsism of art and the struggle for social justice. By the end of his poem, Vallejo comes to a kind of exasperated wail—"How speak of the not-I without crying out." I wanted the poem to have some of the authority and ferocity found in "A Man Walks By . . ." The authority and ferocity of Vallejo's voice are what make me return, again and again, to his poetry.

. . .

DAVID WOJAHN teaches in the MFA Program at Virginia Commonwealth University. His sixth book of poetry is *Spirit Cabinet,* University of Pittsburgh Press (2002). In 2001, he published *Strange Good Fortune: Essays on Contemporary Poetry* with the University of Arkansas Press. Pittsburgh will soon publish his *New & Selected Poems.*

CAROLYNE WRIGHT

Message to César Vallejo

Caught in the crosswind
of my desires, I'm here
to stay: New Orleans,
Crescent City along the river
that still moves underground
to take the dead in its arms.
Where moss creeps down
ropes on the hanging trees,
and the children of mixed blood
carefully whiten the faces
in the photo albums. I hear
the blues through a grillwork door:
I can't go on this way.

Vallejo, you would understand
how a lover's memory of home
opens the shuttered windows,
and know why he still paces off
outlines of the auction block.
How we don't owe any explanation
for where we don't belong.

I read your exile's life again.
Those months in the Chicama Valley
you watched Indians come back at dusk
from the sugar fields for the day's
handful of rice, the sweat of alcohol
on credit, your first poems

burning the plantation storehouse
to the ground. Trujillo's jail
and España falling on its thorns.
Even then you knew
how border towns are everywhere
and the passport that opens them
a switchblade through melons.

No more excuses, you would say.
No listening for the lover's key
in the lock, breath like mosquito netting
I've wrapped myself in.
Suitcases are too easy,
the army blanket from Da Nang
at the foot of the bed
another reason not to stay.

You never went home to Huamachuco.
What you knew Good Friday,
1938, crying those last words
from your bed: "I want to go
to Spain!" as Franco's troops
swept down the Ebro Valley to the sea.

César, I'm staying.
I, whose people starved
during the York enclosures
and burned at the stake

in Zurich, know how often my name
was written in the logbooks
of slave ships. I cancel
the exit visas I thought
my life depended on.

.   .   .

THIS POEM GREW OUT of my reading of Clayton Eshleman's introduction to
César Vallejo: The Complete Posthumous Poetry, translated by Eshleman and José
Rubia Barcia. I was living at the time with a fellow poet and Vietnam veteran in New
Orleans—a city with a history of slavery and an ongoing negotiation with social
and ethnic stratification. Vallejo's poetry had influenced me greatly—when I first
read a bilingual edition of *Trilce* in graduate school—toward a more open-ended,
"surrealistic" mix of dictions and imagistic risk-taking in my own work. The details
I was reading, in New Orleans, of this Peruvian poet's impoverished, transitional,
displaced life impelled me to write a "message" to him—to seek, in his experience,
some revelation or resolution to troubling questions about my own and my then-
partner's family and personal histories and current circumstances. Although Vallejo
could not answer me, the very writing of the poem, as an imaginative entering into
his life, enabled me to stand "in the crosswind" of my own conflicting impulses and
to effect some provisional internal truce.

.   .   .

CAROLYNE WRIGHT has published seven books and chapbooks of poetry; three
volumes of poetry translated from Spanish and Bengali, and a collection of essays.
Her most recent collection is *Seasons of Mangoes and Brainfire* (Eastern Washington
UP / Lynx House Books), winner of the Blue Lynx Prize, the Oklahoma Book Award
in Poetry, and an American Book Award. Forthcoming in 2006 is a new collection,
A Change of Maps (Lost Horse Press). She is on the Board of Directors of the AWP,
and Translation Editor of *Artful Dodge*. After several years of visiting teaching posts
throughout the U. S., she has returned to write and teach in her native Seattle.

CHARLES WRIGHT

from Looking Around II

I sit where I always sit,
                          knockoff Brown Jordan plastic chair,
East-facing, lingering late spring dusk,
Virginia privet and honeysuckle in full-blown bloom and too sweet,
Sky with its glazed look, and half-lidded.
And here's my bat back,
The world resettled and familiar, a self-wrung sigh.

César Vallejo, on nights like this,
His mind in a crash dive from Paris to South America,
Would look from the Luxembourg
                                  Gardens or some rooftop
For the crack, the tiny crack,
In the east that separates one world from the next,
                                           this one from
That one I look for it too.

. . .

I FIRST DISCOVERED VALLEJO—as I did so many things—in Iowa City in the 60s. The poem I was so taken with was one whose title escapes me now. It was merely a listing of nouns, a real tour de force that was clever and moving at the same time. Always a good combination.

He exists as a ghost in my pantheon, rather equivalent to Dino Campana, whom he somewhat resembles, though he is a stronger figure and a better poet I think. They both seem to drift along as spirits to be placated, to fill up a tiny bowl with blood for, as they, both metaphorically and physically, gave so much of it to poetry in their own lives. Little hearth gods, I suppose, who warm our passage.

.   .   .

CHARLES WRIGHT is the author of fourteen collections of poetry, most recently, *A Short History of the Shadow,* Farrar Straus Giroux, 2002. Among his many awards are the Pulitzer Prize, National Book Award, Lenore Marshall Poetry Prize and the Ruth Lilly Poetry Prize.

GARY YOUNG

We buried Sarah's father in the cemetery on Meder Street. He had told his daughter, I'll be dead in three days, and three days later he was—a Thursday without clouds, the year 5762 by his count, but he's past all calculation now. That afternoon we listened to an ancient music: the mourner's Kaddish, the rustle of leaves, and hard earth falling on a casket. It was getting hot; the wind had fallen out of the trees. I stopped at the grave of my old friend Zwerling who once ground the lenses for my glasses in a shed behind his shop. I set a piece of honey-colored marble on one side of his tombstone. On the other side there were other stones—a flat river rock, scraps of granite, a black stone, a white one.

· · ·

I FIRST READ César Vallejo while I was in graduate school thirty years ago. I was struck then by the way his poems obscured the boundaries between the animate and the inanimate, between man and the earth, man and God. The poem that moved me the most, a poem that still haunts me, is "Black Stone Lying on a White Stone." My youthful sensibilities were shaken by the notion that a man could predict his own death with such conviction. As the years have passed, I have seen, more than once, people predict, or perhaps simply will their own death at a prescribed time. My poem, with a nod to Vallejo, describes one such episode.

· · ·

GARY YOUNG has published five collections of poetry, most recently *No Other Life* (2002) which won the William Carlos Williams Award from the Poetry Society of America. Heyday Books will release a new book, *Pleasure*, in 2006. Among his awards are the James D. Phelan Award, a Pushcart Prize, grants from the Vogelstein Foundation, California Arts Council, the National Endowment for the Humanities, and two grants from the National Endowment for the Arts.

ACKNOWLEDGEMENTS

All poems and prose complements in this limited edition anthology are used by courtesy and permission of the individual authors.

Neil Aiken: "A Winter's Day Like Any Other" used by permission of the auhor.

B.H. Boston: "Ars Abstentia" used by permission of the author.

John Bradley: "We Do Not Mourn You, César Vallejo" first appeared in *Poetry East,* used by permission of the author.

Christopher Buckley: "After a Theme by Vallejo, After a Theme by Justice," from *Dark Matter,* 1993, used by permission of the author.

Mark Cox: "Grain" from *Thirty-Seven Years from the Stone,* used by permission of the author.

Ana Delgadillo: "In Veracruz" first appeared in *Sentence,* used by permission of the author.

John Olivares Espinoza: "Black Hair Lying on a White Pillow" first appeared in *SOLO,* used by permission of the author.

Timothy Geiger: "The Black House in Whitehouse, Ohio" used by permission of the author.

Ray Gonzalez: "Fierce God" from *Consideration of the Guitar: New & Selected Poems,* 2005, used by permission of the author.

Anne Gorrick: "Paris: Where All Thursdays Go to Die" used by permission of the author.

Lola Haskins: "Final" appeared in *Extranjera,* 1998, used by permission of the author.

Edward Hirsch: "A Walk With Vallejo in Paris" from *For The Sleepwalkers,* 1981, used by permission of the author.

Richard Jackson: "You Can't Get the Facts Until You Get the Fiction," from *Unauthorized Autobiography,* 2004, used by permission of the author.

Janine Joseph: "Anilao, 1989" used by permission of the author.

Donald Justice: "Variations on a Text by Vallejo" from *Departures,* 1973, used by permission of the author.

George Kalamaras: "Beware the Insistence of Gravity, or Upon Waking in the Body of César Vallejo" from *Heart Without End*, 1986, used by permission of the author.

Jesse Lee Kercheval: "Film Upon Film" first appeared in *Hotel Amerika*, used by permission of the author.

Vandana Khana: "Against Vallejo" from *Train to Agra*, 2001, used by permission of the author.

Ruth Kessler: "After All the Wings of Birds" used by permission of the author.

Justin Lacour: "Variation on Vallejo's Black Stone on a White Stone" used by permission of the author.

Erik Lesniewski: "Brown Stones Under Blue Sky" used by permission of the author.

Philip Levine: "Black Stone on Top of Nothing" from *The Mercy*, 1999, used by permission of the author.

Larry Levis: "The Crimes of the Shade Trees" from *The Afterlife*, by permission of the estate of Larry Levis.

Alexander Long: "Night Sky" used by permission of the author.

Ginny MacKenzie: "Note" used by permission of the author.

Derek McKown: "Belly of the Poet" used by permission of the author.

Victor Olivares: "Chuy out to Sea—Cuba, 1998" used by permission of the author.

C. Mikal Oness: "Family Violence" used by permission of the author.

Robert Philips: "Variation on Vallejo's "Black Stone on a White Stone" first appeared in *Ontario Review*, used by permission of the author.

Brady Rhoades: "Photograph Found Between the Pages of *Los Heraldos Negros*," used by permission of the author.

Doren Robbins: "Before and After Tampico" first appeared in *Caliban*, used by permission of the author.

William Pitt Root: "Vallejo Was Right" first appeared in *Poetry Miscellany*, used by permission of the author.

Dixie Salazar: "Dusty Footsteps" used by permission of the author.

Luis Omar Salinas: "Letter too Late to Vallejo" from *Walking Behind the Spanish*, used by permission of the author.

Rebecca Seiferle: "Oh give me your hand and draw me up from the suffering of this mysterious realm," used by permission of the author.

Pamela Stewart: "My Only Photograph of César Vallejo", from *Cascades*, used by permission of the author.

Jon Veinberg: "Preaching for Winos" used by permission of the author.

David Wojahn: "Ode to 196–" from *The Falling Hour*, used by permission of the author.

Carolyne Wright: "Message to César Vallejo" from *Seasons of Mangoes and Brainfire*, 2005, used by permission of the author.

Charles Wright: from "Looking Around II" from *A Short History of the Shadow*, used by permission of the author and Farrar, Straus and Giroux.

Gary Young: "We buried Sarah's father . . ." from *Pleasure,* 2006, used by permission of the author.